ONLY LOVE CAN MAKE A MIRACLE

Only Love
Can Make a Miracle
The Mahesh Chavda Story

Mahesh Chavda

Published By
Mahesh Chavda
PO Box 411008
Charlotte, NC 28241
Phone: (704) 543-7272
Fax: (704) 541-5300
info@chavdaministries.org
www.chavdaministries.org

Printed in the United States of America
10 digit ISBN 0-9714986-0-1
13 digit ISBN 978-0-9714986-0-0

Originally published by Servant Publications
Cover design by Michael Andaloro
Library of Congress Cataloging-in-Publication Data

Chavda, Mahesh, 1946-
   Only love can make a miracle: the Mahesh Chavda story /
Mahesh Chavda with John Blattner.
   p. cm.
   ISBN 0-89283-674-1
   1. Chavda, Mahesh, 1946-   2. Evangelists—United
States—Biography.   3. Spiritual healing
4. Miracles   I. Blattner, John   II. Title.
BV3785.C516A3 1990
269'.2'092—dc20   90-44771
[B]   CIP

Dedication

"Go back and report ... what you hear and see: The blind receive sight, the lame walk, those who have leprosy are cured, the deaf hear, the dead are raised, and the good news is preached to the poor." Matthew 11:4-5

This book is dedicated to the author of every good report—the Lord Jesus Christ.

Contents

Contents

About the Author

MAHESH CHAVDA and his wife, Bonnie, lead Chavda Ministries International, a worldwide apostolic ministry with a vision to proclaim Christ's kingdom with power, equipping believers for ministry, and ushering in revival.

Raised as a devout Hindu in Mombasa, Kenya, Mahesh came to Christ at the age of sixteen after a dramatic encounter with Jesus. For over forty years, the Chavdas have been reaching the nations with the gospel accompanied by signs, wonders, and miracles. Hundreds of thousands have come to salvation and thousands have received healing from critical diseases such as AIDS and cancer through their ministry. Many of these miracles have been medically documented, including healings from Stage-IV cancer, extreme physical disabilities and ailments, as well as the resurrection from the dead of a six-year-old boy.

In addition, Mahesh and Bonnie have produced many useful tools for believers including this book, *Only Love Can Make a Miracle*, and other titles such as *The Hidden Power of Prayer and Fasting*, *The Power of the Cross: Epicenter of Glory*, *Getting to Know the Holy Spirit*, and many others.

Together, the Chavdas pastor All Nations Church in Fort Mill, SC. They also spearhead the global prayer movement, The Watch of the Lord™, leading their congregation and others around the world in corporate prayer since 1994.

Preface

ONLY LOVE CAN MAKE A MIRACLE is the inspiring and fascinating story of Mahesh Chavda's life and ministry. As such, it recounts how the supernatural power of the kingdom of God and the anointing of the Holy Spirit have characterized Mahesh's call, both in his personal life and in his international ministry of evangelism, healing, miracles, and deliverance.

The reader should be aware that the major healings and miracles cited from Mahesh's ministry have been documented by the testimony of eyewitnesses and, where pertinent, by competent medical authorities. For example, the resurrection from the dead of six-year-old Katshinyi, highlighted in chapters one and fourteen, has been documented by the written and videotaped testimony of the boy's family and the medical staff at the clinic where he was pronounced dead.

In another miraculous incident, Mahesh Chavda led a healing service in Kananga, Zaire and started by binding the work of evil spirits. Seven miles away, witch doctors gathered at the "Sorcerer's Tree" to curse the Christians and their God. Fire is said to have streaked across the sky and struck the tree, demonstrating the power of the God of the Christians.

As explained in chapter thirteen, "That tree stands to this day outside Kananga. It had once been more than thirty feet tall. Now it looks like the remains of a huge match stick, burned from the top down. The trunk is not split, as it likely would have been had it been struck by lightning. The first several feet of the trunk are untouched, which would not be the case if someone standing on the ground had set the fire."

This incident—which is somewhat reminiscent of Elijah, the four hundred and fifty prophets of Baal, and the fiery consumption of the sacrifice to the God of Israel on Mount Carmel in 1 Kings 18—has been documented by the testimony of eyewitnesses and photographs of the tree taken after it was struck. Two of these photographs are included in the photo insert in this book.

For Mahesh, such healings and miracles are not sensational events that should be viewed in isolation; rather, they are meant to herald the gospel of Jesus Christ and bring people into the full freedom of the kingdom of God. They testify to God's love and power in desiring to draw all men and women to himself. As Jesus tells us in Mark 16 before his ascension, "These signs will accompany those who believe: in my name they will drive out demons, they will speak new languages . . . They will lay hands on the sick, and they will recover" (vv. 17-18).

Our sincere prayer is that *Only Love Can Make a Miracle* will inspire you to a greater experience of God's love and a greater faith in his power to work in your life.

ONE

Kasavubu Square

I T WAS MIDDAY. I was in Kinshasa, the capital city of Zaire, in the heart of Africa. I had just finished addressing a crowd of some thirty thousand people gathered in Kasavubu Square in the center of the city. It was the third day of a week-long campaign in Kinshasa, which had somewhat unexpectedly become one of my stops on a two-month-long visit to Africa during the summer of 1985.

Zaire is the modern name of what most people in the West remember as the "Belgian Congo." Though it is a country of great natural beauty, most of the people live in grinding poverty. There is tremendous unemployment. Spiritually, Zaire is still in the grip of witchcraft and sorcery cults that have dominated Africa for centuries.

There may be as many as three million people living in and around Kinshasa. When I first arrived, I had no way of knowing how many of them might be interested in coming to hear a Christian evangelist, with an Indian name, who came from the United States of America.

The invitation had come a few months before, in the form of a letter from a pastor in Kinshasa. When I wrote back and accepted the invitation, I had indicated that I would arrive in Kinshasa on Sunday, June 9. That was the only correspondence I had had with my hosts. I could only hope that the man who invited me would be at the airport to meet me.

He was. As we drove toward town, I inquired about plans for the campaign. "Have you scheduled a seminar for the mornings?"

"Yes, sir," he replied.

"And have you made arrangements for open meetings in the evenings?"

"Yes, sir."

"About how many should we expect at the open meetings?" I was hoping there might be as many as five hundred.

"About fifty thousand, sir."

That took my breath away. "Fifty thousand!" I exclaimed.

"Yes, sir," he said. He seemed almost apologetic. "That is because it is during the week. We will be able to have a big crowd on the weekend."

Obviously, the Lord had more in mind for my time in Zaire than I had anticipated.

It quickly became apparent just how much the Lord did have in store for us. About two thousand attended the first seminar on Monday morning. As I finished speaking, I heard the Holy Spirit tell me that there was a woman in the crowd who was dying of cancer, and to invite her to come forward. An elderly woman, her body covered with cancerous tumors, came walking down the aisle. As she neared the stage, the power of the Holy Spirit came upon her and knocked her to the ground as if by a physical blow. By the time I reached her, the tumors had disappeared. She rose to her feet and went away dancing for joy. The Lord had healed her.

News of this miraculous healing spread like wildfire. That night, instead of the fifty thousand we had expected, almost one hundred thousand people showed up. There were cripples, lepers, people with AIDS. I had never seen anything like it. Some of the sick people were brought to the meeting in wheelbarrows, soaking in their own urine and excrement.

Many cripples were healed that night, including a number

of little children. It is difficult to describe the overwhelming emotion I felt as I saw these little ones walk without canes or crutches for the first time in years, perhaps for the first time in their lives. The manifestation of the power of God was so strong that even avowed witches and sorcerers were repenting and accepting Jesus Christ as their Savior and Lord. For them to take this radical step in public was a spiritual earthquake.

The crowds continued to grow. By Wednesday, there were thirty thousand people just at the morning seminar. It was as though we had moved into a new dimension of the working of the Holy Spirit.

The meeting had started at 9:30 in the morning with singing and worship. I began to preach at 10:30. I finished my talk at the stroke of noon and had just stepped back from the microphone, when I sensed the Holy Spirit speaking to me.

Suddenly, despite the throngs of people milling about, it felt to me as though the world had simply fallen silent, as though time itself had stopped. I saw nothing, felt nothing, heard nothing. I was aware of nothing except the quiet, gentle voice of the Holy Spirit: *"There is a man here whose son died this morning. Invite him to come forward. I want to do something wonderful for him."*

This was far from the first time I had heard the Lord speak to me in this way. Over the years, he had spoken to me many times, sometimes amid large crowds like this, sometimes in intimate settings where I was alone with someone in pain. It was the Holy Spirit's way of telling me how he wanted to work in a given situation. I had learned at such times not to question, not to analyze, but simply to obey. I stepped back to the microphone and said what the Lord had told me to say.

The crowd was buzzing, waiting to see what would happen next. Those who had been present at our earlier meetings had already seen several amazing healings and miracles performed in the name of the Lord Jesus. Yet the people could sense that the Holy Spirit had something special planned for this moment.

A few seconds passed and then a man came running toward the platform. He threaded his way through the crowd, waving his hand in the air and crying, "It is I! It is I!" As he came toward me I studied him. He was tall and built like a boxer. I could see in his eyes a mixture of hope and fear, faith and doubt. I asked him no questions, not even his name. I simply placed my hands on his head and began to pray.

"Lord Jesus, in your name I bind the powers of darkness and death that are at work in this man's son, and I ask you to send your Spirit of resurrection to bring him back to life."

When I finished the man gazed at me for a moment, then nodded his head one time as if to say, "Thank you," and ran off again. The crowd parted to let him pass.

I was not to see him again or learn the full story of what happened for several days. But by the time that evening's service began, we had begun to hear amazing reports about the man who had come forward for prayer.

His name, we learned, was Mulamba Manikai. He had a six-year-old son named Katshinyi. Early that morning, Katshinyi had been pronounced dead by doctors at Kinshasa's Mikondo Clinic. The body was taken to Mama Yemo Hospital. At noon on June 12, 1985, as I prayed for his father in front of thirty thousand people in Kasavubu Square, the little boy suddenly came back to life.

The Lord had raised Katshinyi from the dead.

As I recalled Mulamba threading his way back through the crowd, I remembered another word the Holy Spirit had spoken to me here on this same continent of Africa just a year earlier.

SEEDS OF FAITHFULNESS PRODUCE FRUIT

I was ministering in the remote bush country of northwest Zambia. People from several hundred villages throughout the region had gathered, and the Lord had been at work in marvelous ways.

Late one night I heard a knock at my door. It was one of the missionaries who was sponsoring our visit. "We've just gotten word of a little child in one of the villages who is dying from cerebral malaria," he said. "In fact, he may already have died. But the people there have heard about your healing services. They want to know if you will come and pray for this child."

We left immediately. I knew enough about cerebral malaria to appreciate the seriousness of the situation. The fever could affect the brain. Left untreated, it can kill in 48 hours.

By the time we arrived at the village, the boy had already been dead about an hour. The body was cold and stiff. I took that little boy in my arms and held him close. I sat down in a corner of the family's hut and prayed. For more than an hour I prayed, asking the Lord to bring him back from death, but nothing happened.

I will never forget the crushing sadness I felt as I handed the boy's body back to his mother. With great tears streaming down her cheeks, she looked toward heaven and spoke softly in Lunda, "Now Jesus take him gently with both hands." Then turning to me, "He will no longer run to me. But someday I will go to him."

I stood outside that hut for a long time. I felt so tired and alone. A wind swirled around me, and in the wind I sensed the presence of the Holy Spirit. He said: *"Because you have been faithful, I will let you see great things."*

Now I stood in front of thirty thousand people in Zaire, thinking of the Lord's promise to "do something wonderful" for a man whose son had died that morning. I remembered the Lord's promise that I would "see great things." Was this to be one of them?

The anointing on our meetings in Kinshasa was as great as any I had ever experienced. I felt like I was riding the crest of a tidal wave of God's power. So when I heard the Lord tell me to call forward a man whose son had died that morning, I knew I had been right to obey without hesitating.

I thought of the many other times I had heard the Lord speak to me, when I had seen him act in power. The time when my own son had been hours from death in a hospital in Florida, and the Lord had miraculously preserved his life. The time the Lord first taught me about his healing love, in a school on the plains of West Texas, full of children the rest of the world had cast aside. The time when I, a fatherless Indian boy growing up in the Hindu section of Mombasa, Kenya, had come face to face with the Lord Jesus himself, had felt him place his hand on my shoulder, had heard him call me his little brother.

Nothing the Lord did would surprise me now.

TWO

The Sons of Kings

I WILL ALWAYS TREASURE THE LEGACY my family left me. As I grew up, my mother would tell me, "Don't live like a cockroach! Merely being alive means nothing. Cockroaches and lizards eat, breathe, and die. It's how you live that matters. Make your life count!"

Although he died while I still was a young boy, the memory of my father, Keshavlal Ladhubahai Chavda, preserved and passed on to me through the members of my family, had a great influence on me. His example of integrity as a community leader and defender of the oppressed has shaped my mental and spiritual life.

My father was a striking man, with rich black hair and a full mustache. At five feet ten inches, he was tall for an Indian. He seemed even taller than that because of the magnificent turban he wore on special occasions. Very few Indians knew how to tie the royal turban. To my father, wearing it symbolized the proud ancestry of our family.

A MAN OF HONOR, FAITHFULNESS, AND LOVE

He had been born in Dhoraji, India, December 12, 1893, but had moved to Mombasa, Kenya, when he was twenty-seven years old. Like India, Kenya was then part of the British Empire. My father had obtained a position as a civil servant in the British colonial government. He worked in the educational system. In time, he would rise to the respected position of principal of the Allidina Visram High School in Mombasa. There Indian, Arab, and African boys whose families were British citizens received a "proper" British education.

Mombasa, along the Indian Ocean coast just south of the equator, was a fascinating city. Situated on an island at the southeast corner of the country, it formed a natural seaport. For years the old harbor on the east side of the island was a major crossroads of the British Empire. There goods flowed into and out of the African interior, and the civilizations of East and West met to trade their wares.

In the early 1900s, a new and deeper harbor was built on the southern side of the island, near Kilindini, and most of the major shipping activity moved there. This left the old harbor to Arab sailing ships, called *dhows*, which continued to trade in fruit, dried fish, and goods from India and other Persian Gulf countries.

As often happens with port cities, Mombasa came to be inhabited by men and women representing the seemingly endless array of peoples who had passed through it over the centuries. The Africans who founded the city had been dominated by Arabs during the Middle Ages, then by various European countries during the colonial period. First came the Portuguese. Then, later, the English, who staffed their mercantile and governmental positions with workers and civil servants imported from all corners of the empire—like my father. Mombasa in the 1940s was a bewildering mosaic of races, nationalities, cultures, religions, and languages.

My father had married at the age of thirty. His bride, Laxmiben Pragjibhai Solanki, was fifteen years old, the age at which young women were typically given in marriage. In accordance with the custom of the time, her marriage to my father had been arranged by relatives some years before. It was in 1923 that Keshavlal sailed to Laxmiben's home town of Jamnagar, India, to claim his bride and take her back to Kenya with him.

Our family lived in Mombasa's Kibokoni neighborhood, a predominantly Indian and Hindu enclave located only a few hundred yards from the old harbor. Here Keshavlal and Laxmiben would raise their family of eight children. There were five daughters—Vasanti, Rama, Indu, Mala, and Sheila—and three sons—Vinod, Krishna, and myself. I was the second youngest in the family, having come into the world on January 14, 1946. My parents named me "Mahesh," which is derived from "Mahaishvar," or "Lord of Lords." Literally, it means "devotee of God."

There were few real streets in Kibokoni. Instead an intricate web of narrow, crowded alleyways led to neat stucco homes with tin roofs. Our home was one of the nicer ones in the area, owing to my father's respected position in the community. Downstairs were two bedrooms and a sitting room, three bathrooms, a large kitchen area where we took our meals, and a covered veranda where my mother would sit in the shade through the long, hot afternoons preparing food for the evening meal. The walls were cement and stucco, the floors terrazzo. Upstairs were three bedrooms, one of which was used for the family shrine and one where in later years I would keep my books and the radio on which I would listen every night to news broadcasts from the BBC. The house had electricity and running water.

Not far away was an old military post with the unusual name of Fort Jesus, built by the Portuguese in 1593, to protect the harbor from marauding Arabs. My brother, Krishna, would take me to the fort, where I loved to play, scrambling over the World War I artillery pieces that still stood there and dreaming about the battles that had been waged there through the centuries.

The tropical sea breezes that swept in from the ocean, carrying pungent smells of salt and fish, drew us like magnets to the old harbor itself. Shops and open air markets offering all manner of goods surrounded the harbor where my friends and I would prowl the docks in search of adventure.

This terrified my mother who had been told that the captains of the *dhows* liked to snatch small children and sell them into slavery in faraway lands. We didn't care. We knew better than to get in the way of the wild animals that sometimes wandered into town from the surrounding countryside, and we knew better than to wander into neighborhoods where there were thieves about and a great deal of violence. We knew our way around the old harbor, and we felt safe there.

My father was one of the leading men in Mombasa's Indian community, owing to his professional position, his education—he could read and converse in nine languages, including Persian and Hebrew—and his strength of character. He was a natural leader and was regarded as an elder statesman among his people.

For example, the 1940s were a time of political unrest in Mombasa—indeed, throughout all of Kenya. The powerful Mau Mau guerrillas were agitating for Kenyan independence from the British. They struck terror in the hearts of people all over Kenya. Nerves were on edge and tempers flared easily. Restless crowds, poised for trouble, would take to the streets at the slightest provocation. On one occasion, the unrest spread into our Kibokoni neighborhood. Keshavlal strode into the midst of the gathering mob and called out in Swahili, the local dialect, "Quiet! Quiet! Return to your homes!" That was all it took. The crowd was stilled and in a few moments began to disperse. A potential riot had been averted.

My father—I called him *Bapuji*, meaning, "honored

father"—was descended from India's royal *Rajput* caste. The *Rajput*—literally, the "sons of kings"—were feared warriors, similar in many respects to the orders of knights that developed in medieval Europe. They considered it their sacred duty to defend their homeland and to vindicate the poor, the weak, the defenseless.

The motto and rallying cry of the *Rajput* was simple but profound: "One Word—One Woman—One Sword." One Word—when a member of the *Rajput* gave his word, he kept it. He preserved his honor even if it cost him his life. One Woman—meant a *Rajput* chose one woman, and to her he would be faithful for life. One Sword—the *Rajput* never recklessly sought out a fight, but once a sword was drawn, it was not to be returned to its scabbard without blood on it.

I was raised on stories of the heroic exploits of my *Rajput* ancestors. During the fifteenth and sixteenth centuries, for example, when the hordes of Islam began to swarm into India, it was the *Rajput* who led the resistance. India was then a collection of scattered, independent kingdoms, many of them easily overrun by the superior numbers of the Moslems.

When the Moslems captured a town, they would assemble the entire population and forcibly "convert" them to Islam. They would line the people up and force them to open their mouths while Moslem soldiers walked past and spat into their throats. The alternative was to have their heads cut off on the spot. The *Rajput* would defiantly lay down their lives rather than accept the shame of defeat and renounce their Hindu faith.

My father was not only a leader to the community, he was also a provider and protector of the less fortunate. He always took a personal interest in the welfare of the Africans and Indians who worked with him or for him. He would encourage them to complete their education, to advance in their occupations, to develop themselves as husbands, as fathers, as contributors to the community.

Over the years, he quietly became a father to many who were poor or destitute. His compassion for those less fortunate than himself seemed boundless. After his death, we discovered lists of widows and orphans in Kibokoni and throughout Mombasa whom Keshavlal had supported out of his personal income during the troubled years of the Great Depression—yes, its influence was felt even in East Africa—and World War II. This, too, was part of being a *Rajput.*

In early 1951, my father suffered a stroke. His powerful frame now spent its waking hours lying in bed or folded into a chair on the veranda. The powerful voice that once could quiet street mobs now only whispered.

It was early on the morning of July 18 of that year that I was awakened by a commotion in the house. *Bapuji* had called my sister Rama and asked her to bring him something to drink. When she entered his room she found him slumped over in bed. We summoned a doctor immediately, but it was too late. He was dead.

I was five years old when my father passed away. The events surrounding his death now seem like a distant dream to me—my mother and sisters ceremonially washing the body; my mother at the funeral, dressed all in white; the clamor of wailing and mourning as the flames consumed the funeral pyre.

Kenya's parliament declared a national day of mourning in honor of Keshavlal Ladhubahai Chavda.

Tragically, *Bapuji's* generosity—which had blessed so many during his life—became a great burden to his family after his death. Never anticipating a premature death, he had spent all his extra income on caring for others. He never considered that he might need to provide for his family's future.

As young as I was, I didn't fully realize what all this meant to my mother, to my brothers and sisters, to myself. I would not feel the full impact of being fatherless for some time. It would leave a void, an emptiness in my heart, and I would spend years searching for something—or someone—to fill it.

LEARNING TO BE A KING'S SON

My father had given me a great deal even in the short time we had together. He had given me life. He had given me a name and a destiny. His example taught me that it was not just living that mattered, but how one lived. His legacy had given me a sense of honor, of courage, of duty that comes from being a descendant of the *Rajput,* the "Sons of Kings."

My fascination with my heritage gave birth within me to a fierce sense of honor—which got me into trouble on more than one occasion.

It was not uncommon for gangs of Arab boys to patrol the streets of Mombasa, looking for smaller children to rob. These teenage thugs would spy out children walking alone, corner them, and steal from them everything they had.

One afternoon I was walking home from school when I rounded a corner to find two little boys standing in the street, crying. A gang of four Arab boys—they appeared to be about fifteen years old—were in the process of roughing them up and robbing them. I was younger and smaller than they were. But I was descended from the *Rajput,* and I knew what I had to do.

I marched into the middle of the fracas and demanded loudly, "What's going on here? You can't do this!"

The four thugs looked at me with amusement. "Yes?" they asked. "And what are you going to do about it?"

I had neither numbers, size, nor strength on my side. My only weapon was the element of surprise. In a flash, I grabbed the boy nearest to me by the arm and threw him to the pavement. He skidded across the dirt and gravel, skinning his knees. His wounds were far from mortal. But I had drawn blood!

The other three thugs were so startled by my sudden move that they turned and fled down the street. The two little boys were still so frightened they were unable to offer more than a fleeting, mumbled "Thank you" before they, too, scampered away.

I was still standing there in the middle of the street, pleased with myself for having done my duty, when the four teenagers came back—with reinforcements! I found myself surrounded by a mob of boys—there must have been twenty of them—carrying clubs and chains.

"What do you want?" I asked, though I had a sickening feeling that I knew already.

"We're going to teach you a lesson!" their leader snarled.

"All of you?" I asked. Any one of them looked capable of teaching me more than I felt the need to learn at that moment.

"We're going to make you bleed like you made our friend bleed," one of them cried. They clearly had more in mind than giving me a pair of scraped knees.

As I stood in their midst, one of them would sneak up from behind and hit me with his club. When I turned to face my attacker, another would rush in from behind and strike me on the back or head.

Fortunately for me, all this had only just begun when one of my teachers happened along. Some local shopkeepers, who had heard the disturbance, were with him. While the shopkeepers and the gang members held a rather heated discussion of the merits of street justice, my teacher pulled me aside. "I think it would be wise," he said, "if you got out of here as fast as you can." I was by now beginning to see that discretion might indeed be the better part of valor. I raced home at once.

As the years went by, I would grow wiser in confronting

evil. But I never had any doubt that there was a struggle between good and evil, or about which side I was to take. I began to formulate a picture of a world in which there was no neutral territory, in which those who compromised with evil became its slaves. It was a lesson of spiritual warfare that was to stand me in good stead many times in the years to come.

Indeed, all these things would make a great difference in my life when I became a son of the King of kings, Jesus Christ.

THREE

Search for Truth

T HOUGH MY MOTHER, LAXMIBEN, was small of stature, she seemed to possess a boundless energy that poured out through her shining face, glistening eyes, and ready laugh. *Bapuji's* untimely death had left her facing the seemingly impossible task of providing for her family. His small pension from the British government helped, but it didn't come close to covering our needs. My eldest brother, Vinod, had married and moved away. Had it not been for my middle brother, Krishna, who quit school at age seventeen in order to support us, we would almost certainly have become destitute.

Even so, times were very hard for us. Sometimes Krishna would be unable to find work for periods of time, and we would have to get by on the little bit of money my mother had managed to set aside. I remember many times seeing the pain in her eyes when I told her I was hungry—growing boys are almost always hungry—and she had to tell me that we had no food. My school was about four miles away, and I would walk there and back wearing an old pair of shoes held together by some copper wire I had found. I called them my "crocodile shoes," because of the way the soles and uppers flapped when I walked.

A SENSE OF FAMILY TRADITION

The *Rajput* values my father had held dear were imparted even more strongly by my mother. Maintaining our family tradition of being generous and gracious, despite the difficulties of our financial situation, was important to her. She instilled this value into me at an early age—especially on one memorable occasion.

The *Diwali*, or "Festival of Lights," is one of the most colorful and exciting events on the Hindu calendar. We looked forward to it the way children in the West look forward to Christmas. The days leading up to the festival were filled with the preparation of all types of special foods. Different families would specialize in making certain kinds of dishes: pies, cookies, sweetmeats, or savory dishes hot with curry and other spices. These specialty dishes would be given as gifts to friends and neighbors. Then, when the rounds of visiting began, everyone could serve his guests a sumptuous collection of foods.

The day before the celebration, the family would gather up all the small containers they could find, fill them with oil, and make wicks for them. In the evening as light began to fade, the family would set the lamps outside all around the house, and light the wicks. As the darkness deepened, every home would be surrounded by lamps. There would be hundreds of them, bringing a warm, mellow glow to the entire neighborhood.

But the best part of *Diwali* was the firecrackers. Early on the morning of the festival, the children would jump out of bed, eager to begin setting off the firecrackers they had hoarded for the occasion. Yet the children wouldn't set them off all at once: these noise-makers were precious, and it was important to make them last as long as possible.

Despite our poverty, mother always seemed to find a way to make *Diwali* a celebration. One year, when I was about seven years old, she had taken the extraordinary step of selling some of her jewelry so we could have the traditional foods, and so that I could have a small bag of firecrackers to enjoy. How I treasured those firecrackers! I kept them carefully hidden, checking each day to make sure they were safe and sound.

When the great morning of *Diwali* dawned and the other children began setting off their firecrackers, I waited. Midday came, then afternoon. Still I waited. I was looking ahead to nightfall, when I could enjoy my tiny sackful of firecrackers to the fullest.

Late in the afternoon, after the food gifts had been distributed and the visiting was in full swing, a family of distant relatives stopped at our house. They were quite well off, and their children were, frankly, quite spoiled.

The nine-year-old son was a particular problem. Self-centered and totally undisciplined, he ran around the house at will—breaking things, making noise, and generally ruining the celebration for everyone else. His mother seemed oblivious to his behavior and made only superficial attempts to restrain him.

For my mother to have spoken to the child, or to his mother, would have been out of the question. Guests in Hindu homes were treated with the utmost graciousness. Correcting them, or even denying their slightest desire, was an unthinkable insult that brought dishonor upon the host family.

Inevitably, it happened. In the midst of his flurry of activity, my young guest's eyes fell on the little sack I had so carefully set aside. He peeked inside.

"Mommy, Mommy!" he cried. "Look! Firecrackers! I want to set them off! Ask for me, Mommy. Please, ask for me!"

His mother turned to mine and smiled. "He wants to celebrate *Diwali* like the others. I'm sure you won't mind."

Mother didn't hesitate an instant. She nodded to her guest, then turned to me. "You'll let him have your firecrackers, won't you, son?"

I was too stunned to protest—which would have been an almost unimaginable act of defiance in any case. I slowly and silently handed over the firecrackers to my relative, who ran outside to squander them. They had little value to him, but they were so precious to me! Losing that small sack of firecrackers was as traumatic to me as a child in the West losing an entire year's worth of Christmas presents. It was all I could do to choke back my tears.

Later when the guests had all gone, my mother's arms were full of empathy as she hugged me. "Mahesh," she whispered through her pain, "there is no sadness during the Festival of Lights."

I understood. The honor of our family, the dignity of our heritage, and the obligation to show proper hospitality was of far greater value than a handful of firecrackers. "No, Mother," I said softly. "There is not."

Mother was devoted to us, to the *Rajput* traditions, and to the Hindu religion. She raised us to follow its ways. Every morning she would rise at 5:00 for personal worship. This began with a ceremonial washing, which represented the desire to be cleansed from evil. Then she would pray in the family shrine. The shrine was actually a large, open cabinet that we kept in the central room on the second floor. Its different compartments held images of various Hindu deities such as Rama and Shiva, pictures of Hindu holy men, and copies of the sacred books. By studying these books, worshiping the Hindu gods, and following holy men, it was thought one would come to possess the virtues they taught and represented.

During special festivals, mother would gather the whole family around the shrine and lead us in singing special *slokas* or hymns. These were written in Sanskrit, the ancient religious language of India. Then she would read portions of the holy books: the *Veda*, the *Mahabharata*, the *Bhagavad-Gita*, the *Ramayana*. These are the principal sacred texts of the Hindu religion. They tell the stories of the Hindu trinity: Brahma, the creator; Vishnu, the preserver; and Shiva, the destroyer. They also tell of Krishna, who was an *avatar*, or physical manifestation, of Vishnu, and who led the fight in the great wars between good and evil.

Mother's grasp of the holy writings was remarkable. She became a respected teacher in Mombasa's Hindu community. Our home was often visited by people who came to discuss the holy books and to hear her expound on the stories and teachings. She became unusually well-educated for a woman and was accepted for membership in the Theosophical Society. She was even granted the rare privilege of being allowed to read and teach in public. For the most part, Hindu culture consigns women to cooking, making a home, and serving the men in the family. To be allowed to teach publicly was a high honor, even for a man. For a woman, it was truly extraordinary.

Nowhere did mother take her responsibilities as a religious teacher more seriously than within the family. Conversations around our dinner table often centered on Hindu theology or on the teachings of Theosophy. (Theosophy is a deliberate blending of Western and Eastern religions, with an increasing tendency towards Hinduism, so that, having started in New York City, it rapidly found its true home in India.) She took special care to impart to me a special sense of loyalty to Hindu tradition, to the legacy of the *Rajput*, and to the example of my father. She had named me Mahesh—"devotee of God"— and she took it seriously. She hoped that her instruction and guidance would one day make me an elder statesman in the Hindu community, just as my father had been.

MY FRUSTRATED QUEST FOR TRUTH

One thing that certainly rubbed off on me from both my parents was a love of learning. I became a voracious reader. Every afternoon while other boys were out playing football (or, as we would call it in America, soccer), I would rush home, bound upstairs to my room, and stick my nose in a book. It got to be quite a joke in the family. When I would come downstairs at seven o'clock, after listening to the nightly BBC news broadcast, my sisters would make a great show of greeting me, as though I were a visiting dignitary. "Oh, he even speaks to us!" they would cry.

An elderly lady from the neighborhood once tried to "cure" me of my passion for reading and studying. It was during the *Holi* festival. *Holi* is a holiday somewhat similar to Halloween. During the day, merrymakers would run around throwing paint on each other and going from door to door asking for donations of firewood to be added to the huge bonfire that night at the temple. If the request was refused, the caller was obliged to play a prank on the home. He might throw paint on it, or he might walk off with the front door, to make up for the missing donation of firewood!

One year our neighbor—a tiny wisp of a woman who must have been more than seventy years old—stopped by our home. After smearing everyone with the obligatory paint, she noticed I was not there.

"Where is Mahesh?" she asked.

"Oh, you know him," my mother replied. "He's upstairs reading as usual."

"Reading!" she bellowed. "On *Holi*?" With that she turned and stomped out the door.

Instead of leaving, she snuck around to the rear of the house and climbed up onto the balcony outside my second-floor room. Stealthily, she crept up behind me and rubbed her paint-covered hands all over my face and hair.

"Now," she declared triumphantly, "you will *have* to honor the festival!" With a sigh of resignation, I joined in the celebration.

By now I was a teenager, and I was passionately involved in a search for truth. My search was fueled, no doubt, by a number of things: my parents' constant reminders to make my life count for something, and my seeking to fill the void in my life caused by my father's death; my mother's example of devotion, and the patient, in-depth religious instruction she gave our family; the stories I had heard since childhood about the Hindu holy men who left their families and rejected all thought of personal comfort to hide away in the Himalayas, meditating and searching for truth. It was said that these Hindu saints never discovered truth in universities or ashrams (the Hindu equivalent of a monastery or a community of prayer), they experienced it as perfect light that tied all of life together in an eternal reality.

The Eastern mind understands "truth" somewhat differently than the Western mind. To an Easterner, truth is not simply a series of facts whose accuracy can be tested by scientific experiments. It is not just something you *know*, it is something you *experience*. It is something eternal and unchanging. It transcends the things of this world, which pass away. It is *reality*. When you don't have it, you know it—and when you find it, you know it.

It was only natural that my search for truth began with the Hindu faith so assiduously passed on to me by my mother. Most boys my age seldom visited the temple. In fact, since Hindu worship is centered in the home, on the family or individual level, rather than in public on the congregational level, there is rarely an official reason for ever visiting the temple. But I would regularly go there three times a week to bow down to the images, burn incense, and talk with the priests.

Yet, the more deeply I delved into Hinduism, the more I found its truth to be like smoke: something that seemed to be there until I reached out and tried to lay hold of it. Then, it simply disappeared. It was interesting intellectually. But there seemed to be no *reality* to it.

Though my mother tried to be tolerant and understanding, my growing disenchantment with Hinduism troubled her. Sometimes it led to tension between us.

Because of mother's position of honor as a teacher of the

Hindu religion, our family often hosted some of the holy men who came to Mombasa. I grew increasingly disturbed at the elaborate preparations and extravagant meals that we—who had trouble making ends meet as it was—had to serve for these "men of god." Most distressing of all, however, was the practice of honoring the holy men by bowing as they entered and touching their legs.

I began to object to this practice. "Mother, I cannot do it," I would say. "I cannot bow down to these men."

"Why not?" she would ask. "They are holy men. They have much to teach us. Besides, it is not really the men to whom we bow down, it is to the ideas they represent."

"But to me they do not represent the ideas they teach. They teach great and noble things. Yet they will eat our food and ask for big offerings. I cannot respect such men."

In the end, she would plead with me, "Son, do this for me. If we do not show proper honor to the holy men, it will bring disgrace on our family."

When the holy men would arrive, I would do as my mother asked—for her sake and for the sake of our family honor, not because I was persuaded of the rightness of what was happening. I would bow down and touch their legs even as everything within me screamed, "This is wrong!" Then, having fulfilled my obligation, I would quietly leave the room and have as little as possible to do with them.

Thanks to my incessant reading and study, I was a very successful student. Twice I had been chosen head prefect at my high school—the same school where my father had served as principal many years before. Being chosen head prefect was the highest honor that could be given to a student, and I was the only student in the school's eighty-year history who had been chosen two years in a row. I was the captain of the debating team. I was involved in drama. I received many awards for writing essays and short stories. People commented that I was clearly earmarked to follow in my father's footsteps as one of the leaders of the community.

Yet I was frustrated. I wanted truth. I had searched for it every place I knew to search, but had not found it. Not in academic pursuits. Not in philosophy. Not in living out my heritage as a descendant of the *Rajput*. And certainly not in Hinduism.

One day I walked out of the temple for the last time. I let the door slowly swing shut behind me, looked up to the sky, and said, "God, I believe you exist. Every ounce of my being is telling me that you are real, that you are out there somewhere. But you are not in that temple. I know that. I am never going back in there again. I want to find you. But where?"

Little did I suspect how soon God was to answer my question.

FOUR

The Ultimate Question

A CURIOUS THING HAD BEGUN TO HAPPEN to me when I was about thirteen years old. I had been brought up speaking *Gujarati*, an Indian dialect. That was the language we used around the house, the language my friends and I used when we were together, the language people used in the ordinary course of daily life. Because my father had been multilingual, we were exposed to other languages, especially English, which I was taught as part of my British education. Still *Gujarati* was my native language.

Now, however, that began to change. I mysteriously began to lose the ability to communicate fluently in *Gujarati*. Suddenly, it became easier for me to say things in English. Before long, I found I was thinking in English, even having dreams in English. Sometimes when I tried to talk to someone, I would have to think through what I wanted to say in English, and then translate it into *Gujarati*. It was more than a little awkward to suddenly have my native tongue become my "second language"! I didn't realize at the time that God was preparing my mind to be able to handle something very important that he was going to want me to read—in English.

One afternoon I was surprised to find my seven-year-old niece, Rajesh, standing at the front door of our home accompanied by a woman I had never seen before. The woman's pale skin clearly identified her as a foreigner.

"I'm sorry to trouble you," she said. "But it's so terribly hot outside, and Rajesh was kind enough to invite me here for a drink ..."

"Of course, of course," I replied. "You are welcome in our home. Please sit down. I will get you some water." Hindu tradition demanded that the utmost hospitality be shown to all guests.

When I returned, she introduced herself. "My name is Sid Pierce," she said. "I've been conducting street meetings here in Kibokoni for the children. They come around in the afternoons and I tell them stories. Rajesh was listening to me today and insisted I come to your house for a drink. I'm sorry to arrive unannounced."

"Not at all," I smiled. "What kind of stories are you telling?"

"My husband and I are missionaries," she explained, "Christian missionaries from America. We have come to Mombasa to share our Christian faith with others. I tell the children stories from the Bible."

Like all Hindus, I had a deep respect for anyone who would devote their lives to spiritual matters. It impressed me that someone would give up family and the comforts of home to move to a foreign land for the sake of sharing their beliefs.

Apparently sensing my interest, Mrs. Pierce went on. "We tell the children that God created men and women to know him and to enjoy life. But we sinned against God and lost our fellowship with him. So God sent his Son, Jesus Christ, to become a man and to die the death of a criminal in order to pay the price for our sins. Anyone who will put their trust in Jesus Christ can have their sins forgiven and enjoy fellowship with God."

By now I was getting the impression that this woman was doing more than just telling me about her work with children. She was preaching to me. I had no desire to hear what she was saying. The gods of Hinduism had lost their meaning for me, and I had no wish to trouble myself with this God of the West.

It would be unthinkable to contradict a guest in our home, so I simply, but firmly, ducked the issue. "I understand completely," I said. "I appreciate what you are saying. I, too, am a seeker after truth. Everyone must seek the truth for himself."

Mrs. Pierce had spent enough time around Hindus to know she was being told that her listener had heard enough. She thanked me for the water and rose to leave. As she did, she reached into her bag and pulled out a paperback book. "Here," she said. "Please accept this from me as an expression of gratitude for your hospitality."

I glanced at the title. *New Testament*, it said, *New English Bible.*

"If you are seeking truth," she added, "you will find it in this book."

"Thank you," I said, as she stepped out the door. "I appreciate your kindness. It has been an honor to have you in our home."

Strangely enough, even though I had been educated in the British school system, I had never read the Bible. I had been to the movies to see Cecil B. DeMille's "The Ten Commandments" and also "Ben Hur." That pretty well summed up my familiarity with Bible stories.

I also had very little familiarity with Christianity. I knew there were a few Christians in our area, but I didn't know much about them. There was a Catholic parish not far away called the Church of the Holy Ghost. I had no idea who the Holy Ghost was. When I was a little boy, my friends and I used to laugh about it: "What kind of a church is that? Do they worship ghosts there? Or is it a church for ghosts?" Once when I was a little older, I went inside. I saw priests wearing robes and burning incense, and people bowing down and reciting prayers in a strange language. As far as I could tell, Christian worship was no different from what happened at the Hindu temple!

Besides, I now reasoned, all truth must surely lead to the source of truth and all religions to the one true God. What difference did it make if people called him Vishnu or Allah or Jesus?

After Mrs. Pierce had gone, I flipped through several pages of the Bible she had given me. I turned it over and over in my hands. It didn't look any different from any other book I had seen. Yet her words lingered in my mind: *"If you are seeking truth, you will find it in this book."*

I decided to read some of it. I started at page one, of course, with the Gospel according to Matthew, and then read the Gospels of Mark and Luke.

I was intrigued by Jesus Christ. Most of all, I was touched by his obvious compassion for the poor and the oppressed. This was unlike anything I had experienced in Hinduism.

Hinduism believes in reincarnation and in a concept called *karma. Karma* is understood as a sort of spiritual force generated by one's thoughts, words, and actions. Your *karma* determines the form in which you will return in your next life. Good *karma* results in your coming back as a wise or wealthy or holy person. Bad *karma* results in your coming back as a member of one of the lower castes—or maybe even in subhuman form. You might come back as a dog if you didn't do too well in your previous existence. If you really blew it, you might come back as a flea on the dog. There was no way to have your sins removed or forgiven. There was no escaping your *karma.*

Thus, the attitude of the Hindu holy men toward those who were suffering was that they were simply living out their *karma* and that nothing could—or should—be done for them. You might feel sorry for them, but they were simply paying a penalty they had brought on themselves. The suffering was even good for them, since it might enable them to earn a better *karma* for their next life. Some even felt that to help them would be to interfere with the divine process.

Jesus, on the other hand, didn't set himself apart from the sufferings of people. He cared for them. He got involved on their behalf. He healed their diseases. He put his love into action.

He even *died* for them. I had never before heard about the cross. I knew about torture, about the sufferings that those in authority can impose on others. I lived in a colony and saw injustice around me every day. Jesus endured that kind of treatment willingly, as a demonstration of his love. He maintained his compassion throughout his ordeal: comforting his mother, speaking respectfully to those who sentenced him to die, even asking forgiveness for his executioners. I had never encountered a religious leader like him.

The Gospel of John especially captured my attention. I have since learned that the Bible is a most unusual book in that it is the only book in which the author looks over your shoulder as you are reading and speaks to you. It was as though that very thing was happening when I read John's Gospel. Particular words and phrases would spring up at me as if they were alive.

Right from the very first chapter, John clearly and straightforwardly identifies Jesus as being God. That was a new notion to me. To the degree that I had ever heard about Jesus at all, it was as a holy man, a wise man, an outstanding servant of God—but not as God himself.

Then, in chapter eight, I read where Jesus said, "Then you will know the truth, and the truth will set you free" (Jn 8:32). I thought to myself, "This man is talking about the very thing I've been seeking. Truth. Truth that will set me free. Free from *karma*, from the heavy burden of always trying to make the gods happy and never succeeding."

Then in chapter fourteen I read something that really took

my breath away. Jesus said, "I am the way and the truth and the life" (v. 6). Those words, "*I am the truth*," seemed to burn themselves into my soul. I felt as though scales were falling from my eyes. All my life I had been searching for the truth, but I had always understood truth as something abstract and impersonal. Now it came home to me that the truth could be a person, a person named Jesus Christ.

The ultimate question, it seemed to me, was whether or not Jesus was telling the truth, whether he was an honest man. I had read enough about him by now to know that there was no in-between with Jesus. With Jesus, everything was either black or white. Either I had to recognize him as being exactly who he said he was, or I had to take him as a total liar.

I thought back over all that I had read about Jesus: his life, his teaching, his miracles, his compassion, his death. Suddenly it seemed unmistakably obvious to me that if there was only one honest man who had ever lived, it was Jesus Christ. If ever there was a man of utter truth, it was him. I remembered something Jesus had said just a few lines before: "In my Father's house are many rooms; *if it were not so, I would have told you*" (Jn 14:2, emphasis mine). I thought to myself, "Well, of course. He only tells us what is so. If it were different, he would have told us. He wouldn't mislead us."

I suddenly began to feel like Pilate. I remembered from my earlier reading how Jesus had stood before Pilate and how Pilate had sneered at him, "Truth? What is truth?" Could it have been that the truth—the ultimate truth, the source of all truth—was standing in front of him even as he asked the question? And was that very same personification of truth now standing before me through the words of John's Gospel? I remembered what Mrs. Pierce had said as she handed me the Bible: "*If you are seeking the truth, you will find it in this book.*" Had I indeed found what I had been seeking so long, in the person of Jesus Christ?

No sooner had these thoughts formed in my mind than

something deep within me seemed to rise up and cry, "No!" The years spent studying the Hindu faith and listening to stories of the holy men . . . the hours spent around the family shrine, and at the dinner table listening to my mother, and in the temple, . . . the proud heritage of my family and my people loomed before me. *"You don't need to go this way,"* it seemed to be saying to me. *"There are many ways to God. You have your own way. You don't need this new way."*

"But I know I have not found the truth in Hinduism," I said to myself. "And I know Jesus is the truth."

"You'll be a traitor," the inner voice seemed to reply. *"You'll be a traitor to your people, to your faith, to your family."*

It was true. I could not deny it. So many people had invested so much hope in me, had such expectations for my life. I was the star student at my school, the one who was to grow up to be a leader in the community, like my father before me. If I chose Jesus Christ, I would be the first in my family— and I could trace my lineage back more than eight hundred years—to renounce Hinduism. I would be turning my back on my ancestors. On my *Rajput* heritage of defending the faith. On my own father and mother!

I was torn in two. The choice before me was painfully obvious: to accept the one whom I now believed to be the embodiment of the truth, even at the cost of losing so much that was precious to me, or to be faithful to my heritage, even at the cost of rejecting him. For months I lived in torment.

Then, one night, I decided the time had come to make a decision once and for all.

FIVE

"My Little Brother"

I N THE END, I DECIDED I simply couldn't walk away from it all: my family, my training, my heritage. Part of me wanted Jesus, but I couldn't bring myself to pay the price. And I couldn't take the double-mindedness any more.

For months now I had lived in agony. I would read the Gospels and find myself so attracted to Jesus that the next step—committing my all to him—seemed obvious and easy. Then the pull would go the other way, as I thought of the heartache I would cause my friends and family.

Finally, I had had enough. It was late one night. I was upstairs in my second-floor bedroom reading my Bible as I usually did. I was sitting at my desk, with a bed sheet wrapped around my body, pulled up over my head, and snuggled around my face so that my eyes could just peer out. I had to do this because of the mosquitoes swarming around me. The mosquitoes were horrible in that part of Africa, and in those days we had no window screens and, of course, no spray cans of insect repellent.

My moment of decision had arrived at last. "No more," I said to myself. "Enough is enough. I am never going to think about Jesus Christ again." I despaired, thinking about leaving behind the one who, I knew, loved me so much, but I didn't waver. I slowly, firmly closed the Bible. "I am never going to read this book again," I said. "My mind is made up."

And that was that.

Or so I thought.

The next thing I knew, I heard my head hit the desk. I mean I literally *heard* it, as if it were happening to someone else. *Bang.* I seemed to be in a sort of half-sleep, no longer fully awake and in control, but aware of what was going on. I remember hearing the noise and thinking to myself, "That's my head, hitting the desk."

I immediately found myself in a strange and wonderful place. My body was still there at the desk, but in my spirit I was somewhere different, somewhere wonderful, somewhere I had never been before. The thought came into my consciousness, very simply and clearly, "I am in heaven."

Up until this time, I had not read any of the New Testament except the Gospels. I was so enamored of Jesus that I just read them and reread them, over and over. I had never read the Acts of the Apostles or the Revelation or any of Paul's letters. If I had, I would have come across a passage in Paul's Second Letter to the Corinthians that would have helped me understand what was happening to me. Speaking of himself, he writes:

> I know a man in Christ who fourteen years ago was caught up to the third heaven. Whether it was in the body or out of the body I do not know—God knows. And I know that this man—whether in the body or apart from the body I do not know, but God knows—was caught up to Paradise. He heard inexpressible things, things that man is not permitted to tell.
> 2 Cor 12:2-4

I don't know whether what happened to me was exactly the same as what happened to Paul. I do know that what happened to me was unmistakably real. To this day, I sometimes find the Lord bringing back to my consciousness things that I experienced that night. They are just as real to me now as they were then.

The first thing I noticed was that I was walking on a street or pathway of some sort that appeared to be made of gold. It was different from any gold I had ever seen before. It seemed to be clear. You could almost see through it. Years later I read that when scientists purify gold with atomic particles, it becomes translucent. That's what the gold on this pathway was like, as though it had been thoroughly purified.

Along both sides of the path was luxurious grass, like a thick blanket that you could lie down on and fall asleep. There were trees and flowers of every size and description. The colors were fantastic: yellows, greens, golds, blues, pinks—more colors and shades than I could have imagined. The quality of the color was unlike anything I had seen before. On earth, the colors we see are because of reflected light: light strikes objects from the outside, and depending on their molecular structure, they reflect particular spectrums of that light back to our eyes which perceive them as the various colors.

These colors were different. It was as though they provided their own color from within. The light wasn't reflecting off of them, it was pulsating from inside them, an absolutely pure light. To this day, when I see colors on earth—even spectacular ones—they seem tainted or faded to me.

I became aware that I was hearing music. At least, it was more like music than anything else I had ever experienced. It was as though the grandest symphony orchestra and the most splendid choir ever assembled were performing—though I could not distinguish particular instruments or voices. It was glorious.

I found my whole being dancing in keeping with the music. It was as though every one of my senses was perfectly harmonized with it. In fact, my overall sense was one of complete harmony, of perfection, of the total integration of everything around me—the vegetation, the light, the colors, the music. They were distinguishable from one another, and yet in utter unity with one another, all at the same time.

I was somehow part of it: part of the splendor, part of the harmony, part of the perfection. I wasn't just seeing and hearing and smelling what was around me. I was integrated into it. I didn't just experience joy and love and purity and harmony, I somehow became part of them, and they became part of me.

I felt that I was *home*. This was where I wanted to be, where I was *supposed* to be. This was why I had been created.

For the first time, I noticed a sort of river flowing alongside the pathway where I was walking. I say, "sort of a river," because it looked like a river, but between its banks was flowing something unlike any water I had ever seen. At first, it seemed as though the water were alive. Then I realized that the "water" actually *was* life itself. It was literally a river of life. Again, though I didn't realize it at the time, the Bible describes just such a river. During his amazing vision of heaven, the Apostle John writes,

> Then the angel showed me the river of the water of life, as clear as crystal, flowing from the throne of God and of the Lamb down the middle of the great street of the city. On each side of the river stood the tree of life, . . . Rv 22:1-2

I SAW JESUS

Suddenly, I became aware of a brilliant white light coming toward me. I turned and saw a man walking toward me. I knew immediately who it was. It was Jesus.

Now bear in mind that I had never seen a depiction of Jesus. Most people who grow up in the West see many artistic representations of what Jesus might have looked like. Some of these are based on scraps of historical data that are still in existence. Some, I suppose, are drawn primarily from the artist's imagination. I had never seen such renderings of Jesus. On the natural plane, I had no idea what he looked like. Yet there was not a trace of doubt in my mind that the man now walking toward me was him.

On the one hand, he looked like a normal human being. Average height. Average build. He was walking normally along the same pathway I was on, wearing an ordinary-looking long robe, not unlike those I had seen many times on Arab men in Mombasa. And yet...

I was almost blinded by the light that was streaming forth from him. It was bright and pure and alive, as if it contained the fullness of heavenly glory. I could hardly look at him.

I remembered the accounts I had read in the Gospels of the time Jesus took Peter, James, and John up the mountain to pray. Mark writes that Jesus "was transfigured before them. His clothes became dazzling white, whiter than anyone in the world could bleach them" (Mk 9:2-3). All the accounts especially mention the blinding light. Matthew says of Jesus: "His face shone like the sun, and his clothes became as white as the light" (Mt 17:2). Luke writes that "his clothes became as bright as a flash of lightning" (Lk 9:29), and says that in looking upon Jesus, his disciples "saw his glory" (v. 32). I felt as though I knew just what the writers of the Gospels were talking about.

As he came closer to me, I could see that he was smiling. It was the same kind of smile you see on the face of a mother or father when they pick up their little baby, a smile of utter love and delight. Like a moth flying into the flame, I felt as though I was going to be instantaneously consumed by pure love.

He came closer still, and I saw his eyes. I will never forget the eyes of Jesus. I could see that those eyes had felt every hurt, every heartache, that had ever been felt. They had shed every tear that had ever been wept on earth. Yet they were not eyes of sadness or gloom. They were eyes of triumph, eyes that seemed to say, "Yes, I know the pain, I know the heartache, I know the tears. I took it all upon myself when I died on the cross. But I have overcome. And you can overcome, too."

Then as I stood there gazing into his eyes, he stretched out his hand and placed it on my shoulder and said to me, simply, "My little brother."

As suddenly as it had begun, it ended. I was once again on the second floor of my house with my bed sheet drawn around my face and my head resting on my Bible—but something strange had happened. When all this had started, when my head had fallen forward onto the desk, my Bible had been closed. I had just made a decision never to open it again. Now, however, it was open. I looked down and saw that it was opened to chapter eighteen of Luke's Gospel, the story of the rich young ruler.

I realized at once how similar I was to this anonymous young man. Like him, I had been groomed to be a leader among my people. Like him, I had diligently sought after the truth. Like him, I had been led to Jesus in the course of my searching and had asked Jesus to make the truth plain to me. Like him, I had stood face to face with Jesus himself. I had seen Jesus look upon me with love. I had heard Jesus call me to follow him.

I knew how the story ended. The young man had turned away from Jesus with inexpressible sadness in his heart because he could not bring himself to pay the price of becoming Jesus' disciple.

I heard a voice within say to me, "Are you going to turn away from me the same way he did?"

I said, "No, sir."

Then I did something that, to my knowledge, no ancestor of mine had ever done, that no one in all the eight hundred years of our family history could even have imagined doing. I got down on my knees and said, "Jesus, I'm sorry. Please forgive me for all the wrong things I've done. I want you. I want to give my life to you. Please come and live in my heart."

I got up and looked around. It had been about ten o'clock at night when I had closed my Bible and my head had fallen forward onto the desk. It was still dark outside, but it felt as though several hours had passed. About an hour later, I began to hear the roosters crowing, which ordinarily happened at about 4:30 in the morning. I realized that the whole experience had taken place over the course of several hours. It wasn't like one of those experiences you sometimes have, when a long string of events seems to flash through your mind in an instant. Apparently, it had happened in real time, and I had been "gone" for several hours.

When I got up off my knees, I felt... different. I don't know whether people who grow up in the Western world fully appreciate the revolutionary quality of the gospel. We have churches on every corner, Bibles in every hotel room, and holidays on our calendars whose Christian background we take for granted. Christianity just seems to become part of the "cultural wallpaper." We don't know what a radical transformation the gospel can make in a person's life when it is embraced in all its reality.

I knew that I was thoroughly changed. It would take time for me to grasp all the implications of what had happened to me. There was a lot I didn't know about being a Christian, but I did know that I had entered into eternal life. I knew I was born again. I knew that God was my Father, that Jesus was my Lord, and that heaven was my home. Most of all I knew that the weight of my sins, which had been so apparent till now, was totally gone!

I knew that everything in life would be different from now on. In the next few months, I would find out just how different.

SIX

A Visit from an Angel

I HAD NEVER SEEN SUCH RAIN.

It was nine o'clock in the evening. I was making my way home from the library at Texas Tech University, in the city of Lubbock, where I was enrolled as a graduate student in English Literature. I had a deadline coming up on an important research paper, and I had been holed up in the library since ten o'clock that morning.

My apartment was about a six-block walk from that part of campus. "Apartment" is a charitable word for it. It was really more like a shack: one main room with a couch and a television set at one end and a bed and dresser at the other, a small kitchen area, and a tiny bathroom. It stood in one of the more run-down of Lubbock's many run-down neighborhoods. As I think back on it now, it was a pretty grim place to live. But it was all I could afford, and I felt lucky to have it.

When I had gone into the library that morning, it had been just another of the dry, hot days that was pretty much the norm for Lubbock in May. But things had changed dramatically since then. Not that sudden storms were uncommon on the west Texas plains. Without warning, it seemed, huge storm clouds hundreds of feet high would come boiling up out of the west and roll through bringing heavy rains and high winds. Then, as suddenly as they had appeared, they vanished.

This storm, for some reason, felt different. The rain was pounding harder, the wind gusting more fiercely, the air felt heavy. I was already drenched. I couldn't wait to get home and get out of the rain.

When I was growing up in Kenya, I suppose that Lubbock, Texas, would have been one of the last places on earth I would ever have imagined myself living. But my extraordinary encounter with the Lord that night in my bedroom in Mombasa, and my subsequent decision to commit my life to him, had changed my life in many ways that I could not have anticipated.

The morning after the encounter with Jesus in my bedroom, I excitedly told my family what had happened. My younger sister, Sheila, was the only one who seemed at all intrigued by what had happened to me. It happened to be Sunday morning. Sheila, who had continued to drop in on Mrs. Pierce's neighborhood Bible classes, told me that Sunday was the day when the missionaries had their church services. We went to church that morning, and I renewed my acquaintance with the Pierces. They didn't quite know what to make of my story, but were glad to see my obvious interest in Christianity. They invited me to come back. I did, several Sundays in a row. I also started meeting with the Pierces during the week. We had many fascinating discussions about the Bible and about the new faith I had adopted.

The Pierces, I learned, were from Texas. They called themselves "Baptists." That was the first time I had known that Christians came in different varieties. I didn't really know what a Baptist was, except that I was familiar with John the Baptist from my reading of the Gospels. The missionaries explained to me not only about Baptists but also about water baptism, which—they showed me from the Bible—was an essential part of my new Christian life.

It was also the straw that broke the camel's back as far as my mother was concerned. She had listened quietly to my account of my late-night encounter with Jesus, but she showed no desire to hear more about it. I could tell she was troubled and hurt by my obvious enthusiasm for the Christian God. But if she wanted to say anything to dissuade me from the course I was pursuing, she held her tongue.

Now, however, when I told her I intended to be baptized, she was devastated. This, she knew, was a definite and unmistakable outward sign that I was rejecting Hinduism and pledging myself to the Western God. There would be no turning back, and we both knew it. She was wise enough, however, to realize that it would do no good to object or to try to change my mind. So in April of 1962, I was baptized in the water of the Indian Ocean, near Mombasa's old harbor where I had played so often as a little boy.

I was nearing the end of high school, and it was time for me to think about what to do after graduation. For as long as I could remember, I had longed to go on to college, perhaps to one of the great universities in England that I had heard mentioned in such reverential tones at the Allidina Visram High School.

The missionaries, seeing my studious nature and my intellectual curiosity about Christianity, were urging me to consider Bible college. I had no interest in entering the ministry, but I was eager to learn more about Jesus and the Bible. In time, they persuaded me to apply to Wayland Baptist College in a place called Plainview, Texas. I was not only accepted, I was offered a full scholarship. A Baptist church in Texas had heard about me and had collected enough money to pay for my plane fare. So, in January 1964, I left Mombasa and headed for the United States.

AN ANGEL IN DISGUISE?

I laugh now when I think of what I must have looked like the day I arrived in New York. It was the dead of winter, of course, but I had never experienced winter before, so I knew nothing about cold weather. I had no coat. I had almost no money.

As it turned out, I discovered that I also had no plane ticket to Texas. My flight had gone from Mombasa to London and then across the Atlantic to New York. I was supposed to catch a flight to Dallas, then go on to Lubbock, and then to Plainview. Apparently somewhere along the way, some airline employee had inadvertently ripped one too many coupons from my book of tickets. I was stranded at the airport in New York City with seven American dollars in my pocket and not the foggiest idea of where to go or what to do next.

I wandered around the huge terminal building for a while. Then I decided to step outside. What a shock! It was bitter cold and a thick, wet snow was falling. Having gone from tropical to northerly temperatures within several hours since leaving Africa, I stood there in my suit, shivering. I would have turned around and gone back inside, but I was transfixed by the incredible number of cars whirring past. I could stand on a street in Mombasa for hours and not see as many cars as were flying past me here in the space of ten minutes.

Finally, I went back inside. I was miserable. I was wet. I was cold. I was stranded in New York. I was all alone.

Just then, something remarkable happened. A man appeared as if from nowhere—a big man, expensively dressed, wearing a pair of shiny cowboy boots and a ten-gallon hat. He put his arm around my shoulder and said, "Say there, son, you look like you're lost."

"Yes," I said. "I know I bought a ticket but the airline people say I don't have one, and I don't have any money and I don't know what to do."

"Where are you headed?" he asked.

"To Lubbock, Texas," I said. "Well, actually, first to Dallas."

"Dallas?" he cried out. "Why, that's where I'm going. You just wait right here. You're coming with me."

His name, he told me, was Jack. He went up to the counter and bought me another ticket, and the next thing I knew, I was on my way to Dallas. There were some people from the college waiting to meet me at the airport in Dallas. When Jack saw them, he said simply, "Take care of yourself, son," and walked off. I never saw him again.

Plainview, Texas, had a population of about fifty thousand people and the most appropriate name I had ever heard for a town. I enrolled at Wayland College for the winter semester. I took Bible, of course, but also literature, philosophy, and other subjects. Wayland was fundamentalist in its doctrine and quite strait-laced in its behavior code, both of which were fine by me.

DISCOVERING CHRISTIANITY IN AMERICA

During the sixties, West Texas, like many areas of the United States, was coming to a crossroads in its racial attitudes. Even the influence of staunch Bible-belt fundamentalism had not kept it from the infection of prejudice. As an Indian from Africa, I was considered something of a novelty and had little trouble fitting into the predominantly white culture. However, I quickly saw that the same could not be said for blacks.

One night an elderly black man knocked at the kitchen door of a restaurant where I worked part-time. "Sir," he asked, "can you fix me a meal? I'm hungry."

It seemed a strange request. "You know, this is a restaurant," I told him. "Why don't you just go around front and order what you want from the menu?"

"Oh, no sir," he said. "I wouldn't want to cause any trouble."

I realized the problem was that this old black gentleman would not be welcome in the restaurant. "Well, come on in, then," I said to him. "You sit down here in the kitchen. I'm going to make you the best steak you ever ate." And I did. I suppose it was lucky for me the manager never found out. I might have been fired.

In Kenya we had people of all races and backgrounds: Indians, Africans, Arabs, and others from around the vast British Empire. Different groups had their own cultures—to be sure—and often their own neighborhoods. Somehow I had assumed that it would be different here in the "land of the free."

I soon learned that this prejudice even existed on campus. A friend of mine, a young black man, received the news that his mother was dying. Understandably, he was distraught. His friends rallied to support and comfort him. One of the people who befriended him was a young lady in his classes. She was white. The fact that they began keeping company on campus came to the unhappy attention of a certain member of the student administration, who was also a minister. My friend was called in to this fellow's office and returned in tears.

"What's the matter?" I asked him. I was afraid he had been told that his mother had died.

"I was warned to stop hanging around with a white girl or risk losing my scholarship," he said.

I couldn't believe my ears. My *Rajput* temper flared. I marched straight to that fellow's office. "I thought you people were Christians," I shouted at him. "This poor guy's mother is dying. He's barely hanging on. And you—a *minister*—treat him like this? How can you do something like that?"

"Let me explain something to you," he said. "We're not putting up with any trouble. You are here on scholarship yourself. One more outburst like this, and I will personally see to it that your scholarship is revoked. From now on mind your own business."

Going to church in America was very different from the lively times I had shared with the missionaries in Africa. In those services, I had sat next to lepers and blind men and children so poor they couldn't afford shoes. Still they all were in love with Jesus and loved to sing his praises. Now I sat next to people who wore nice clothes and nice smiles and were born and raised in the church and surely would know, I thought, what it meant to be Christians.

As far as I could see, their idea of being a Christian mostly meant being somber and serious. We would sing a serious hymn, pray a serious prayer, listen to a serious sermon, take up a very serious collection, and get a serious handshake at the door as we left. Inside I was shouting, "No, no, you don't get it. It's Jesus! He's wonderful! He's glorious! He's alive! Aren't you excited?" A couple times I shared my testimony and said how disappointed I was at the deadness I saw around me in the church. People would just pat me on the head and say, "Well, you're new. You'll settle down in time."

By the time I finished my degree—a major in English, a minor in history—I was thoroughly disenchanted with the church. I still loved Jesus and honored him as my Lord, but was disillusioned with Christianity as I knew it. For a while, I got involved in political movements looking for a cause to devote myself to. But in the end, in my heart I knew political movements would never heal the world's ills.

After graduating from Wayland College, I enrolled at Texas Tech University in Lubbock, about sixty miles away. My goal was to get a doctorate in English literature. Money was, as always, a problem. I would work at various part-time jobs until I could afford to take a couple of classes. Then I'd cut back on my work hours for a semester and try to rake up a few credit hours. It was a grueling and tedious lifestyle. During one of these periods, I found myself wearily trudging home from the library late one evening amidst a torrential rainstorm.

THE EYE OF THE STORM

I was glad to get inside, away from the ominous weather. I dropped my books and my raincoat in a heap on the floor, and then dropped myself in a heap on the ragged old couch that was my main piece of furniture. I reached over and clicked on my tiny black-and-white portable TV. It was an ABC special called "The Eye of the Storm." I was so tired. I just wanted to watch TV for a few minutes before I called it a day.

Suddenly, all the lights went out. The TV went black, of course, and so did my whole apartment. "Terrific," I muttered. "Now I can't even find my way over to the bed." I decided just to sack out there on the couch, at least until the power came back on. I slumped back and closed my eyes.

At once I was jolted awake by what sounded for all the world like a voice. "*Get up,*" it said.

I must be hearing things, I thought. I must have studied too long. I must have fallen asleep and dreamed that I heard a voice.

"*Get up!*"

I sat up with a start. I certainly wasn't sleeping that time. But who . . . ? I looked back over one shoulder, then the other. By now my eyes had adjusted to the darkness, but there was no one there—at least, no one I could see.

It came a third time. A very clear, very calm voice, speaking to me in the darkness. Again the insistent message: "*Get up!*"

All at once, I felt something—someone?—begin to push me up off the couch. I was wide awake now! What in the name of heaven was happening? I tried to resist, but it was no use. I felt myself being pushed until I was all the way around the back of the couch and down on the floor. I lay there, gripping the top of the couch, trying to fight back, trying to pull myself up, but there was nothing I could do.

Then it happened. I heard a sound like a hundred freight trains roaring through the front yard, then a loud crashing noise, and a sudden stabbing pain in my left hand.

Twenty-six people were killed and two thousand injured in the killer tornado that hit Lubbock on May 11, 1970— many of them right in the part of town where I lived. It was considered one of the deadliest days in Texas history. The morning light revealed scenes of utter devastation. The tornado had cut a swath one-and-a-half miles wide and eight miles long. Hundreds of cars lay flattened. Hundreds of homes were demolished and thousands were damaged, leaving many homeless. Many of the places I was so familiar with were now nothing more than piles of rubble.

In one area of Lubbock, called "Guadalupe," two policemen found an open Bible amidst the ruins. The wind had left the Bible open at Psalm 83: "So pursue them with your tempest and terrify them with your storm. Let them know that you, whose name is the LORD—that you alone are the Most High over all the earth" (Ps 83:15, 18).

When morning came, I discovered that the crashing noise I had heard was a pane of glass that had been blown out of my front door and sent sailing through the room like a deadly frisbee. I found a sizeable chunk of it still embedded in the wall, just above the spot where I was lying on the floor. Apparently, it had just skimmed across the top of the couch, in the process cutting my hand. With a chill, I realized that had I still been sitting there, the pane of glass would have decapitated me.

I thought about the mysterious voice that had warned me to get up and about the invisible force that had pushed me, kicking and fighting all the way, to safety. I had heard a little about angels, but no one had ever told me to expect to run into one!

Still, there was no denying what had happened. To this day, I have a scar next to the first knuckle of my left hand where that flying piece of glass cut me—the one that would have killed me, had the Lord not sent his angel to protect me. True, by this time I had largely given up on the church, but I had never given up on Jesus. Evidently, he had not given up on me either.

SEVEN

"Could You Heal My Mother?"

WHEN I WAS IN GRADUATE SCHOOL, **the other students and I** used to joke that higher education was largely a process of learning more and more about less and less. I found this to be true in my own case. Certainly by this time I had become a bona-fide expert at making simple things complicated. I was pursuing a doctorate in English literature.

I still believed in Jesus, but I had become disenchanted with the church and didn't allow my Christianity to play a very important role in my life day to day. I was so busy keeping up with classes and scraping together enough money to live on I didn't have time or energy for much of anything else.

A TORNADO OF THE SPIRIT

It was under these circumstances that I received a letter that had much the same effect on my spirit as the Lubbock tornado had on the city. It was from my brother, Krishna. It said that our mother was dying, apparently from a type of bone cancer.

Mother was now living in London. She and the rest of the family had moved there in 1968 when civil unrest in many parts of East Africa was making life difficult, and even dangerous. These were the years when many former European colonies were seeking their independence. Though my parents were originally from India, they had both become British citizens and held British passports. It was hard for Mother to leave the familiar sights and sounds of Mombasa, to say nothing of the many friends she had there, but moving to London seemed the wisest thing to do.

I had not seen her, of course, since coming to America years before. We hadn't talked on the telephone much; it was too expensive. We did exchange occasional letters. Even that level of communication was somewhat strained, though, since Mother still had not completely reconciled herself to the idea that I had forsaken my heritage, become a Christian, and gone off alone to the United States.

Despite all that, the ties between a mother and a son are strong and enduring. I still loved her dearly, and she still loved me. Now she was terminally ill, my brother said, and was asking to see me one last time before she died.

The problem was, I had no money. Since the day I arrived in the United States, I never had more than just enough funds to make it from one day to the next. I had seven dollars in my pocket the day I landed in New York. The day I received my brother's letter, I had twenty-four dollars. That's not much progress in seven years!

The money I made from working a seemingly endless string of part-time jobs went to pay for my education and to my landlord. I ate a lot of peanut butter in those days and a lot of eggs. Eggs were cheap, and I learned that there were dozens of different ways to prepare them. In view of my circumstances, buying a plane ticket to London was out of the question. I just didn't have the money, nor did I have any way to come up with it on such short notice.

It nearly broke my heart. Every time I thought about my

brother's letter—and it seemed as though I thought about it continuously—I would think of my mother, whom I hadn't seen for so many years. In my mind's eye I would see her there on her sickbed in London, her tiny frame emaciated from the cancer. I would picture her lips forming my name, calling out for me, knowing the end was near, wanting to see her youngest boy just once more.

Everything in me wanted to go to her, to rush to her side and hold her close and tell her how much I loved her. I longed to tell her of the One who loved her even more than I ever could, the One who even now was standing by her side, calling her to himself, yearning for her, wanting her to surrender her life to his loving lordship.

I remembered the face of Jesus, as I had seen it so clearly on that Saturday night in my bedroom in Kenya, years before, when the Lord had revealed himself to me. I remembered his eyes—the eyes that looked as though they had cried every tear that had ever been cried on earth. I knew Jesus had compassion for her now.

I would think of all these things, and I would weep. For days I wept. I would be sitting in class, and the professor would ask a question and call on me to answer. I would stand up and say, "Well, sir, you see ...," and suddenly I would just burst into tears. I was simply overcome with grief for my mother and with shame and frustration at my inability to do anything for her, or even to go and be with her. I felt that I was at the end of my rope, the end of my resources, the end of my very self. I had nothing to draw on for my own strength and support, let alone to offer to others. I did not realize, though, that it was God who was breaking me, so he could fill me with his love.

ANOTHER TASTE OF PARADISE

This went on for three days. At the end of the third day, I came home, flopped down on the bed in my little apartment, and cried myself to sleep.

Suddenly, I found myself in the same place I had "visited in the Spirit" that night in Mombasa so many years before. It was all the same: the pathway of burnished gold, the living river, the amazing music, the luminescent colors.

Again, I saw Jesus. This time I was kneeling before him, with my hands folded in front of my chest, gazing up into those infinitely compassionate, infinitely joyful eyes. He reached out both arms and laid his hands on my shoulders.

As he did, I began to sing. I didn't know what I was singing. I didn't recognize the tune, nor did I know the words. I was just singing. Somehow I knew that it was his touch upon my shoulders that had put the singing inside me.

When I woke up, I was lying on my bed with my hands clasped in front of me. I was praying. I had never awakened in this position before. I got up from the bed. The memory of my encounter with Jesus was still fresh in my mind. I felt as though I just *had* to pray. So I began, simply saying, "Jesus..."

That was as far as I got. All at once, the door to my room flew open. What felt like a strong gust of wind surged into the room. It took my breath away for a moment.

Then, something very strange started happening inside me. It began as a sort of tickling in my stomach—like the "butterflies" feeling you get when you're nervous or excited—but this was different. It felt like water bubbling up, as though there were some kind of hidden spring, deep in my being, beginning to come alive. It got stronger and stronger, bubbling like a brook. It was unusual and wonderful and frightening all at the same time.

In a matter of moments, it felt as though whatever was bubbling inside me wanted to come bubbling *out* of me. I tried to contain it, but I couldn't. If I didn't release it, I felt as though I would just explode. I opened my mouth. As I did, a song came flowing out of me, a beautiful song, a song I had heard only once before: that very night, when I had knelt before Jesus and gazed into his eyes and felt the touch of his hands upon my shoulders.

I still didn't recognize the tune, nor had I ever heard the words. In fact, I had never even heard words like these before. I was familiar with a number of languages. I knew English, of course, and had grown up speaking Swahili, which is the main language in East Africa, and Gujarati—the Indian dialect used in the Hindu section of Mombasa. I knew some Hindi as well, and some Urdu, and even a little German. The words I was singing now, however, didn't come from any of those languages.

Whatever language I was speaking, I was now speaking it quite fluently! It just seemed to come pouring out of me. I was singing at the top of my voice. The more I sang, the more the strange bubbling sensation seemed to grow, and the more it grew, the more I wanted to sing.

The intellectual side of me was embarrassed by what was going on. Here I was, a grown man, a student in graduate school, babbling away like an infant in a language I didn't even know. I started to argue with myself, as though I were two different people. "This is weird," I thought. *"Yes, but it feels so good."* "What if someone comes by and hears me carrying on like this? They'll think I've gone crazy." *"I don't care what anyone thinks. This is wonderful. I don't ever want it to end."* "I really must stop doing this." *"Okay, okay, I'll just keep singing for five more minutes, and then I won't do it any more."*

"Five more minutes," I thought. When I next looked down at my wristwatch, I discovered I had been singing like that, at the top of my lungs, for an hour and twenty minutes. I was in ecstasy. I was more in love with Jesus than I had ever been. I knew he was alive. I just *knew* it.

I was mightily puzzled, however, about the whole experience. What had happened to me was wonderful, but just exactly what had happened to me? I'd never seen or heard of anything like it.

There was a woman in one of my classes at Texas Tech who

was a Catholic nun. Her name was Sister Marsha. Perhaps she could help me understand what was going on.

I got to class extra early the next day. Sister Marsha was already there, seated at her desk, reading a book. I sheepishly approached her and asked if I could speak with her for a few moments. I began to explain to her what had happened: how I had seen Jesus place his hands on my shoulders, the strange bubbling sensation, the uncontrollable singing. Finally, I said, "Well, that's what happened. What do you think? Am I going crazy?"

Sister Marsha's eyes had been growing larger and larger as I was recounting my experience. Now she jumped up from her desk and began to hop up and down, clapping her hands excitedly. "Oh, praise the Lord, praise the Lord!" she cried. "Mahesh, you've been baptized in the Holy Ghost!"

I didn't have the faintest idea what she was talking about. I had never heard anyone use the expression, "baptized in the Holy Ghost" before. I had heard of the Holy Spirit, of course. I knew that he was one of the three persons of the Trinity, and that he had played an important role in creation. I knew that Jesus spoke of him in the Gospels from time to time, and that he had powerfully changed the lives of Jesus' followers after his death, resurrection, and ascension.

I had read the story of Pentecost in Acts 2: the sound of a mighty wind, the tongues of fire, the speaking in strange languages. But it had never occurred to me that what happened back then could have anything to do with what was happening to me now. In fact, I had been taught rather emphatically that what happened back then *didn't* happen anymore.

Yet, according to Sister Marsha, it *did*. The Holy Spirit still came to people just as he did in Acts 2, with the same results: a fresh experience of the reality of God, a new outpouring of spiritual power, and the strange and marvelous ability to "speak in other tongues as the Spirit enabled them" (Acts 2:4). The language in which I had sung so exuberantly for more than an hour that day in my apartment was, according to Sister Marsha, my own personal prayer language, known only to the Lord and me.

Over the next several weeks, I began attending week-night prayer meetings all over the Lubbock area, where I met dozens of people who had also had the experience of being "baptized in the Holy Spirit." They told me more about Pentecost and about the *charismata* or "gifts of the Spirit."

I felt like I was in heaven. One of the main things I noticed was that the Bible seemed to come alive. I had not been a very consistent Scripture reader for the last couple years, but now I couldn't get enough of the Bible. The words of Scripture seemed to jump off the page and burn themselves into my consciousness.

One day I was reading the book of Hebrews and I came to chapter thirteen. My attention was arrested by verse eight: "Jesus Christ is the same yesterday and today and forever." I stared at the words, turning them over and over in my mind. Deep within me, I felt the familiar "bubbling" sensation. What was the Holy Spirit trying to tell me?

JESUS CAN AND DOES HEAL!

"Jesus Christ is the same yesterday and today and forever." I realized that Jesus, who was alive two thousand years ago, was alive today and had not changed one bit in all that time. Everything he did then, he was still doing today: like forgiving sins, lifting up the downtrodden, feeding the hungry, and healing the sick.

Healing the sick. The sudden thought took my breath away. Jesus had always healed those who were sick, even those who were close to death. There were times, the Gospels said, when whole towns would come to him, bringing all those who were sick, and every single one of them would be made well. Could it be possible that he was still doing this today? Could it be possible that he might even . . . ?

I swallowed hard. "Lord," I said, "could you heal . . . my mother?"

Instantly I sensed his answer, like a still, small voice deep inside me: "Pray for her."

Pray for her? But how? "Lord," I said, "how can I pray for her? She is in London, and I am in Texas."

"There is no distance in my Spirit," the Lord seemed to say. "Pray for your mother. Ask me to heal her."

I had never done anything like this before. I didn't know what to say. So I simply said, "Lord, please heal my mother." It was not the most eloquent prayer ever prayed, but it was all I could think of at the moment.

Evidently, it was good enough for the Holy Spirit. About two weeks later, I got another letter from my brother. Our mother, he said, had amazingly recovered from her illness. The doctors could find no trace of disease anywhere in her body. All this happened in 1972. My mother is still alive and well today, well into her seventies.

At the time, neither my mother nor anyone else in the family knew what to make of her remarkable recovery—but I knew what had happened. The Lord had healed her, by the power of his Spirit, released through my prayer. Not long after, my mother, too, came to know of the Lord who had loved her enough to heal her diseases and spare her life. She received Jesus as her Savior and Lord.

In baptizing me in the Holy Spirit and in prompting me to pray for my mother's healing, the Lord had awakened me from a sort of spiritual slumber. Though I did not realize it at the time, he had opened a new door for me. In the coming days, he was to lead me through that door, into a dimension of life in the Spirit I had never imagined.

EIGHT

The School of the Spirit

I WAS LIKE A SPONGE in those early days of being baptized in the Spirit, thirsty for every little bit of understanding I could glean about the Spirit and how he worked, and eager for every opportunity to be where he was at work. Sister Marsha had introduced me to a couple of charismatic prayer meetings in the Lubbock area, which I attended faithfully. I also started going back to church.

The main thing I learned was just how little I knew about the Holy Spirit. He had always been a rather vague figure to me. It seemed to me that Jesus gave the key to understanding the Spirit's role when, at his own "premiere performance" at the synagogue in Nazareth, he proclaimed these lines from the prophet Isaiah:

> The Spirit of the Lord is on me,
>   because he has anointed me to preach good
>   news to the poor.
>
> He has sent me to proclaim freedom for the
>   prisoners and recovery of sight for the blind,
>   to release the oppressed,
>   to proclaim the year of the Lord's favor. Lk 4:18-19

When the Spirit of the Lord comes to us, I realized, he anoints us to go and do the works of God the Father: preaching the gospel, healing the sick, setting the captives free. What did that mean for *me*? What was the Lord anointing *me* to do? Where was he sending me?

The answer, when it came to me in prayer, was surprising. I was regularly asking the Lord, "Where do you want me to go?" One morning, in 1972, he literally awakened me from sleep with the almost overwhelming conviction that I was to go to work at the Lubbock State School for Retarded Children.

This was certainly not what I had expected, but the more I sought the Lord for clarity about his call on my life, the stronger the sense grew. "*I am a father to the fatherless,*" the Lord seemed to say, "*and I am commissioning you. I am sending you as my ambassador of love to these little ones whom the world has forgotten.*"

A woman in one of the prayer meetings I attended was an employee at the State School. When I told her of my sense from the Lord, she was very excited and immediately arranged for me to have an interview there.

The Lubbock State School is located a few miles outside of town. The setting is rather desolate, as is the school itself: a cluster of about fifteen small, squat, concrete-and-cinderblock buildings, surrounded by a high chain-link fence. Here and there were a few shrubs and a sapling or two. My first impression was that it looked like a minimum-security prison.

The children who lived there were tragic cases. Some had been born to mothers who had been using heroin. Some were children of abusive parents. Many were born with some kind of horrible birth defect. All were severely retarded. I remember seeing boys and girls as old as twenty-five, whose mental age was less than one year. Some, despite their size and age, spent all their time in oversized baby cribs where they would remain for the rest of their lives.

The children who came here truly were forgotten by the world. They were wards of the state. In most cases, they had simply been discarded by their parents. Many were never visited by anyone, not even on their birthday, not even on Christmas. The Lord reminded me of his word in Scripture:

> Can a mother forget the baby at her breast and have no compassion on the child she has borne? Though she may forget, I will not forget you! Is 49:15

The day I went for my interview, I was given a tour of the facility. I was introduced to one little boy whose family had, for several years, kept him locked inside a chicken pen. Apparently, it was the only way they knew to keep him contained. He thought he was a chicken and used to walk around the grounds flapping his arms and cackling like a hen. I was also shown the work of the "Phantom Smearer," who used to deface the sides of the buildings by smearing them with feces when no one was looking.

Each dormitory building housed as many as thirty children grouped together according to their mental age and functional level. For some bizarre reason, the different dorms were named after flowers.

The most memorable dorms for me were the ones named, of all things, "Lily" and "Rose." In these buildings lived children whose mental age ranged from one-and-a-half to three years. Many had almost no control over their bodily functions and had to wear diapers. The stench inside these dorms was unbelievable. I am quite sensitive to smells, and I couldn't wait to get out.

That night I prayed a prayer that was not very spiritual but was straight from my heart: "Lord, I know you are sending me to the State School. I'm going to obey you. But Lord, please don't send me to Lily or Rose. I cannot take the smell. Send me anywhere else, Lord, but not there."

Do I even need to tell you what happened? The next day at orientation, the chief administrator said to me, "Mahesh, we've seen you with the children and you're so good with them. We really think you can make a contribution in Lily." I thought, *"Thanks a lot, Lord."*

So I started work as an attendant, while still pursuing my graduate studies in English part-time. Soon, however, I was assigned to a psychology task force, involved in what was called "operant conditioning." We would take simple tasks that we wanted to train the children to do, break them down into minute steps, and then teach them those steps one at a time. We gave positive reinforcement when they did well so they would feel rewarded. In this way, over a period of months, we might teach them how to put on their shirt or their underwear, or how to go to the bathroom.

That was what was happening at the natural level. At the spiritual level, it was another matter entirely. As I came to realize, the State School was my own personal "school of the Spirit." It was my training ground for ministry, my Bible college, my seminary.

ONLY LOVE CAN MAKE A MIRACLE

The Lord gave me an overwhelming love for these children. It was hard to explain. It was as though the Lord broke off a little piece of his heart and placed it inside me. I loved those children as though they were my own. Before long even the smell didn't bother me anymore.

I used to work a nine-hour shift in Lily, usually with the ambulatory children—those who were able to get around on their own. When I was off duty, I would go to the nonambulatory wards just to be with the children there. I had such a love for them. The thought of them having to spend the rest of their lives in those cribs almost broke my heart.

I knew that God loved them, too, and that he wanted to channel that love through me. I didn't really know what to do with them or even how to pray for them. I used to just hold them and pray quietly in the Spirit. Often I would sit in a rocking chair with one of them for hours, just praying and singing in tongues.

One little girl especially touched my heart. Her name was Laura. Laura's mother had been using hard drugs during pregnancy, and she had been born blind and severely retarded. I used to rotate through the different nonambulatory wards on my after-hours visits, but in time I began to gravitate more and more to little Laura. She was so precious to me.

One day I had occasion to go into Laura's ward during the day. It had now been several weeks since I had started holding her and praying with her. As I approached her crib, she turned toward me and stretched out her hands to welcome me! There were a number of staff members nearby. They were amazed. They kept saying to each other, "Did you see that?" Laura had never shown any outward response to anyone before, not even to being touched. Now she was responding to me from across the room. Could it be that she was gaining her sight? Could it be that the Lord was healing her ... through my prayers?

Not long after this, I had a similar experience with a little boy who had been born with a terrible birth defect. His spine was deformed so that he was unable to sit up. Again, after I had been praying with him over a period of several weeks, he suddenly became able to sit up. His back was healed!

As far as I can recall, I never once specifically prayed that these children be healed. I had prayed that way for my mother because I felt the Lord had told me to. Other than that, prayer for healing was not something I was accustomed to doing. When I was with the children, I would simply hold them and pray that the Lord would somehow enable them to experience his love through me. I was as surprised as anyone when they started getting better.

I was already learning many lessons in my school of the

Spirit. My initial encounter with Sister Marsha had already taught me that the Lord works through men and women of every Christian background. Here I was, a Hindu boy converted to Christianity by Baptist missionaries, learning about the things of the Spirit from a Roman Catholic nun! Since then, I have never disdained any of the churches, nor had any problem with learning about the Lord through any of them.

Now I was learning that the power of God was to be found in the *love* of God. When the Lord sent me to the State School, he did not say, "I am sending you as my ambassador of power" or "of miracles." He said, "I am sending you as my ambassador of *love*." That was the way I saw myself and that was the way I prayed for the children: that the Lord would make his love real to them. The healings came almost as a by-product. I learned that only love can make a miracle.

I learned another lesson, too, that has been very important to me through the years. It is that when I am confronted with human tragedy and suffering, I never ask the Lord, "Why?"

It was often very tempting, when I was sitting there in my rocking chair, holding an eight-year-old child with serious physical defects and severe mental impairment, to get upset with God. "How could you let this happen? What kind of God are you, anyway?"

I came to see that this kind of thinking flows from a humanistic frame of mind, not from a genuine knowledge of God. Who was I to stamp my foot and shake my fist at God, as though he were not measuring up to my standards? I was his ambassador, not the other way around. It was not up to me to judge him.

During those long hours of prayer, the Lord would say to me, "Just praise me." As I would do so, singing or praying quietly in tongues, he would help me see that the tragedy and heartache all around me was the work of the evil one, of Satan, not of the Lord. It is Satan who seeks to kill and destroy human beings. God desires their good. We, as God's ambassadors, are commissioned to bring his love into every painful situation so that he can overcome the work of the devil.

A SOBERING LESSON

Yet I still had a lot to learn. For one thing, I was not yet practiced in hearing the Spirit speak to me, in being led and guided by him moment-to-moment. In one case, my failure to heed his call was nearly tragic.

It was two o'clock in the afternoon. I had gone to Lily, one of the boys' dorms, to work for the afternoon. As I was going about my business, I sensed a voice inside me saying, *"Go back to Rose."*

It didn't occur to me at first what was happening. I didn't realize it was the Holy Spirit speaking to me. I thought it was just a random idea floating through my head. I had already been at Rose that morning and saw no reason to go back. So I shrugged it off and kept working.

A few moments later, the voice came back. *"Go back to Rose."* This time I realized it was the voice of the Lord.

Now I am not in the habit of talking back to the Lord, at least not in the sense of being rebellious. Yet I was busy and a little flustered, and so I got a little bit irritated. "Lord," I said, "I've already been to Rose. I was over there all morning. I need to get some things done here at Lily."

There was a pause. Then I heard it again, quite insistent this time. *"Go back to Rose—now!"*

As quickly as I could, I put down what I was doing, asked my co-workers to excuse me, and scurried across the grounds to Rose dormitory. The scene that greeted me was frightening.

The State School had a "foster grandparents" program in which retired couples from the area could "adopt" a student and take him or her under their wing—come to visit the child, bring the child presents on his or her birthday, and so on. One of the little girls who lived in Rose had been spending the afternoon with her foster grandmother. The little girl's name was Helen. She was about fourteen years old.

It had come time for the foster grandmother to leave, so she had brought Helen back to the dorm and dropped her off inside. The problem was that she had dropped her off in the wrong place. She didn't realize that the room she had left Helen in was the room we used for isolating students whose behavior had been dangerous or disruptive.

On this particular occasion, we had had to isolate an older girl, in her twenties, who had had a negative reaction to her medication and had become violent. Suddenly, Helen was in there with her, all alone. The older girl saw Helen and went on a rampage. Helen was terrified. She wanted to cry out, to alert someone to her situation, but she couldn't. Helen was a deaf-mute. She was unable to speak, let alone to scream.

When one of the attendants came by for a routine check on the isolation room, he found the older girl savagely beating Helen with a shoe. Helen's face was a mass of welts and cuts and bruises. There were huge tears streaming down her face as she had wept in silent terror and agony.

When I walked in the door, Helen was surrounded by teachers and attendants and nurses trying to comfort her, putting ice packs on her face to ease her pain. I felt a sharp stab in my heart. Now I knew why the Lord had been telling me to "go back to Rose," and I hadn't listened!

I sat down by Helen's bedside, looking down into those big, frightened eyes. Her face was swollen and purple from the mauling she had received.

"Hi, Helen," I said. "I love you. Do you realize that?" I couldn't help but wonder: if I had responded to the Lord more speedily, could I have prevented this awful thing from happening? "I really do love you," I went on. "And that's not all. Jesus loves you, too."

The moment I said those words, a total peace came into the room. It was as though someone I could not see were suddenly there bringing that peace. I also felt a strange sensation in my right hand. It was a sort of tingly feeling, as if something—some sort of power, or energy—was flowing out of it.

I kept praying. Within a matter of seconds, the appearance of Helen's face began to change. The places that had been black and blue—literally black and blue—turned a deep red, then a lighter red, then pink, and then a perfectly normal skin tone. It couldn't have taken more than two minutes in all. I had never seen the Lord do something so dramatic in such a short time. He had reversed the effects of the savage beating and healed this precious little girl—right before our eyes!

The nurse and the attendants who were watching all this were amazed. They kept saying over and over to one another, "Did you see that? Did you see that?" I shared their amazement. But I didn't say anything. I just stood there silently for a moment, then turned and walked away. I was overcome with emotion. The Lord had taught me a vital lesson, and I vowed in that moment never to forget it. Never again would I delay when I heard the voice of the Lord telling me to do something.

NINE

By Prayer and Fasting

W HEN THE LORD SENT ME TO WORK at the State School for Retarded Children, one of the Scripture passages he gave me, which summarized the manner in which he wanted to work there, was from Psalm 27. It was as though it were a prayer that the Lord wanted to answer for the children in the school:

Hear my voice when I call, O LORD;
    be merciful to me and answer me.
My heart says of you, "Seek his face!"
    Your face, LORD, I will seek.
Do not hide your face from me,
    do not turn your servant away in anger;
    you have been my helper.
Do not reject me or forsake me,
    O God my Savior.
Though my father and mother forsake me,
    the LORD will receive me. Ps 27:7-10

It seemed to me that these children—though they could not possibly understand it, let alone express it—were, in some mysterious way, seeking the Lord's face. They had indeed been rejected and forsaken, perhaps more so than anyone else I had ever known.

Yet despite their severe handicaps, something deep inside them seemed to instinctively respond to the Lord's love, his tenderness, his mercy. The more I allowed the Spirit to flow through me, the more they seemed to receive from the Lord. Often the changes were very subtle and took place over a long period of time. On other occasions, however, the Lord's work was far more immediate and dramatic. Sometimes it was almost frightening.

THE CASE OF STEVIE

One of the most heart-rending cases in the entire school was a boy named Stevie. He had an extreme form of Down's Syndrome ("mongolism"). He was sixteen years old, but his mental age was under two years.

Stevie was what we called a "banger." In more clinical terminology, he was a self-mutilator. Something drove him to put his fists together and beat himself savagely about the head and face. He did this almost continually. His entire face was like one massive callous from the years of pounding. His skin was as thick and coarse as alligator hide. His ears were enlarged and grotesque, his eyes swollen shut, his lips blackened and disfigured. I was asked to develop an operant conditioning program to get Stevie to stop hitting himself.

What could I do? The staff, I learned, had already tried everything they could think of to bring Stevie's bizarre behavior to a halt. His records showed that for a time he had been approved for electro-shock therapy. This was an extreme form of negative reinforcement. Stevie would be connected to a series of electrodes. Whenever he would bang himself, he would receive an electric shock. The idea was that, in time, he would make a connection between the undesired behavior (banging) and the painful consequence (electric shock) and give up the undesired behavior.

It didn't work that way with Stevie. In fact, over the six months or so that this therapy had been attempted, the records seemed to indicate that his self-mutilation had gotten worse, not better. So the electro-shock treatments were discontinued.

Finally, in desperation, the staff had come up with a crude but effective way to prevent Stevie from hitting himself. They fastened his arms to long, rigid splints that kept them fully extended at all times. He would walk around the school with his arms sticking straight out to the side, like the wings of an airplane.

This worked fairly well, except for one thing. It didn't take long for some of the other children to realize how vulnerable Stevie was when he was all trussed up in this fashion. They developed a sort of game: one of the bigger boys would sneak up behind Stevie and give him a push which would send him tumbling forward. Since he couldn't put his arms out in front of him to break his fall, he would land face-first on the concrete. The children thought this was extremely funny.

I really didn't know what to do with Stevie. After so many other things had been tried and had failed, what was I going to be able to devise? Still I noticed the same unusual phenomenon with Stevie that I had seen with so many of the other children: he seemed to experience something of God's love through me and so was strangely attracted to me. When he was with me, he would seem to calm down, to be more at peace with himself. The terrible "banging" would subside for awhile. Yet it never stopped completely; and when he wasn't with me, it was worse than ever.

One day Stevie came running to me after a round of the children's cruel "game." Someone had shoved him face-forward on the playground. His nose was broken and his lower lip was split open. Blood and tears and dirt were running down his face. He threw himself into my arms, sobbing uncontrollably.

I was so confused and frustrated I just didn't know what to do. "Lord," I prayed, "you have sent me here as your ambassador of love to these children. What about Stevie? He just can't go on this way. How can I show him your love in a way that will make a *difference* for him?"

No sooner had I prayed than I heard the voice of the Holy Spirit deep within me. He said to me simply, *"This kind can come out only by prayer and fasting."*

I knew immediately where I had heard those words before. In the ninth chapter of the Gospel of Mark, Jesus is confronted by a man whose son is afflicted by an evil spirit. The boy's father explains that whenever the demon "seizes him, it throws him to the ground ... It has often thrown him into fire or water to kill him" (Mk 9:18, 22).

It seems that Jesus' disciples had been trying for some time to get rid of the demon, but without success. Jesus rebukes the evil spirit: "'You deaf and dumb spirit,' he said, 'I command you, come out of him and never enter him again.' The spirit shrieked, convulsed him violently, and came out" (Mk 9:25-26). Later, when the disciples ask why their own efforts at driving out the demon had been so unsuccessful, Jesus explains, "This kind can come out only by prayer and fasting" (Mk 9:29).

I cannot say I took much comfort from all this. The Gospel story certainly seemed to parallel Stevie's situation in a number of ways. Like the young man in the Gospel account, Stevie seemed bent on self-destruction. Like the disciples in the story, those of us on the staff had tried everything we knew to help him, without success.

Yet the boy in the Gospel story wasn't just sick or mentally retarded. He didn't have a genetic defect, like Down's Syndrome. He was oppressed by an *evil spirit*. Could it actually be that Stevie ...?

Mahesh's father, Kashavlal Chavda, strikes an imposing figure in his royal turban, following the tradition of his ancestors, the Rajput "sons of kings."

Mahesh at age four. Shown here with long hair, he received his first haircut at five years of age in his ancestral home in India, following Rajput tradition.

Kashavlal and Laxmiben Chavda, Mahesh's father and mother, pose for their wedding portrait. At the time of their marriage, which was arranged according to Hindu tradition, Kashavlal was thirty and Laxmiben, fourteen years of age.

A serious student throughout his school years, Mahesh, at age fourteen, receives one of many scholastic achievement awards.

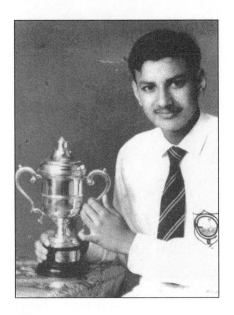

In response to his newfound faith in Jesus, Mahesh, age sixteen, is baptized by a missionary on Nyali Beach in Mombasa, Kenya.

At age eighteen, Mahesh leaves behind his family and his native country of Kenya to pursue studies at Wayland Baptist University in Plainview, Texas.

An aerial view of the path of destruction left in the wake of the infamous tornado that struck Lubbock, Texas, on May 11, 1970. Roofless apartment complexes, businesses, and family homes, partially collapsed or completely gutted buildings, and mounds of debris on empty lots tell the story of this night of terror in which twenty-six persons lost their lives and at least two thousand persons were injured.

With heavy earth-moving equipment on the scene, the city of Lubbock digs out after the May 11 tornado. Mahesh, who was living in Lubbock at the time of the tornado, had to repair the glass panel in his own front door. During the tornado, the entire panel sliced across the top of the couch where he had been sitting only moments before a voice told him to "Get up!" Mahesh believes he may well have been visited by an angel.

"He who finds a wife finds a good thing." Mahesh, as a pastor at age thirty, weds rancher's daughter Bonnie Elkins at Interfaith Church in Levelland, Texas, on July 18, 1976.

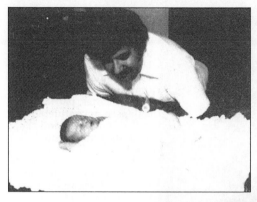

The proud papa and his apparently healthy firstborn, Benjamin, at two weeks old. Benjamin had just been dedicated to the Lord. The next morning he would be rushed to a hospital emergency room and begin a five-month battle for survival against a birth defect, which threatened the collapse of his kidneys and his very life.

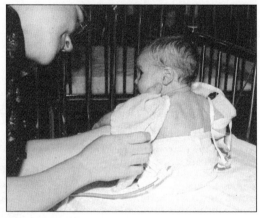

Benjamin at approximately one month old. Having undergone several surgeries, this photo shows surgical bandages and protruding nephrostomy tubes that had been inserted to drain Benjamin's tiny kidneys. The tubes would remain in place until he was seven months old.

Healthy and strong, with his kidneys restored, Benjamin poses in his school uniform at nine years of age.

Aaron Chavda, two weeks after his premature birth, weighing a mere one pound, three ounces. Arriving fifteen weeks premature, Aaron, upon delivery, uttered three tiny mews like those of a newborn kitten!

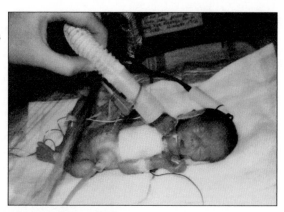

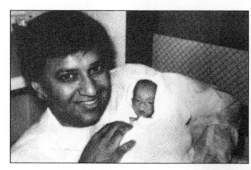

Mahesh returns from Africa, where Katshinyi had just been raised from the dead, to discover that his own tiny son, Aaron, is still alive and making steady progress. Aaron is seen here still in the neonatal intensive care unit at Plantation General Hospital in Fort Lauderdale, Florida. He was two months old.

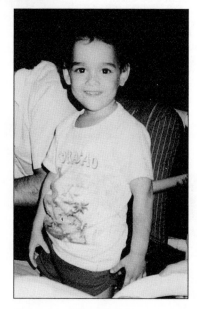

At three years of age, a happy and healthy Aaron plays outside his home in Fort Lauderdale.

Expressing the passion of his life, Mahesh proclaims the gospel to an audience of thousands in Africa. Preaching here about the blood of Jesus, Mahesh believes that Scripture shows signs and wonders are meant to follow the preaching of the gospel.

"You shall lay hands on the sick and they shall recover..." As part of his campaigns, Mahesh holds all-day healing services to minister to the sick through the laying on of hands. The people, who come with every kind of infirmity, are here seated in rows on the ground. Mahesh lays hands on each person in turn at these services and has prayed for as many as seventeen thousand persons in a single day.

A close-up photo of Mahesh at work during an all-day healing service.

Mahesh took this picture of a sixty-year-old woman who was born blind and was sitting alone during a campaign in Pakistan. His heart went out to her since she epitomized the condition of the nations: sitting in darkness waiting for the light of Christ.

At the end of his message that evening, Mahesh said, "Now Lord Jesus, show these people that the message of the Gospel is true." In a moment, from out of the shadows, came that same blind woman, but now she could see clearly. She testified that when Mahesh spoke, she suddenly saw a brilliant flash of light, her eyes were opened to see.

Mahesh holding aloft one of hundreds of children who have been born to formerly barren women after prayer for healing. This baby was named "Mahesh Moke" (Little Mahesh) in honor of God having sent his servant to bless this child's parents.

"Go back and report what you see and hear, the blind receive sight, the cripples walk, the lepers are cleansed, and the good news is preached to the poor." A formerly lame woman walks without her crutches in Zaire.

A young girl brings up her formerly lame brother who was healed at a campaign in the Cameroons. He is shown here running across the platform with one of the local pastors.

Braces and crutches left behind during a campaign in the bush of Zambia.

Mulamba Manikai holds his son Katshinyi. The boy had died of cerebral malaria and was raised from the dead four days prior to the taking of this picture.

"There were added to their number three thousand souls..." Local pastors help Mahesh baptize three thousand persons in one day in the Zaire River during the 1987 campaign.

Approximately half a million people around the world have received Jesus as Lord and Savior through Mahesh Chavda Ministries in campaigns like this one in Kisangani, Zaire.

Having come to Christ through the gift of a Bible from missionaries, Mahesh distributes free Bibles to new converts and others who do not have a Bible of their own.

The African team, made up of local pastors, businessmen, and three members of Mahesh Chavda Ministries Branche d' Afrique, "the African Branch." This photo was taken during the Kinshasa campaign in 1990.

At a site located between the southern hemisphere's largest Hindu temple and Chatworth's Rajput Center, Mahesh proclaimed the gospel under this 12,000-seat tent in Durban, South Africa, in 1990. Ten thousand former Hindus and Moslems made decisions for Christ during this campaign, which was sponsored by the group Jesus for Africa.

Moslem and Hindu Pakistanis listen as Mahesh preaches the gospel in Karachi.

Mahesh prays over a large crowd at the 1988 Milagros (Miracles) Outreach in San Jose, Costa Rica.

Mahesh leads hundreds in receiving the baptism in the Holy Spirit in Zagreb, Yugoslavia.

Pastor Kabanga, vice-president of the Assemblies of God of Zaire, burns a bundle of charms and witchcraft potions brought forward by individuals who had renounced sorcery and received Christ during the 1989 Kinshasa campaign.

Pastor M'Poy Muambi stands at the foot of the "Sorcerer's Tree" of Kananga, Zaire. What is now only a charred trunk was once a huge tree with a thirty-foot limb span. Sorcerers from the entire region would congregate beneath it to cast spells and literally bargain for human lives.

Mahesh and local pastors verify the tree was burned from the top down. Eyewitnesses testify that a stream of fire came through the sky from the site of the campaign grounds during the last evening rally in 1986. The fire struck the top of the tree and proceeded to consume most of it, burning for three days.

The Manikai family and Mahesh outside Mikondo Clinic in Zaire with physician Iwanga Embun, who confirmed Katshinyi's death at the clinic in 1985.

Mahesh visits the Manikai family in Mikondo, Zaire, in 1986, the year after Katshinyi was raised from the dead.

Mahesh with the children from the church which has sprung up in Mikondo through the efforts of the Manikai family after Katshinyi's resurrection.

C.S.S.P.

C. A. D. Z.

Av. Kileyi No 10 Q. Mikondo

Zone de KIMBANSEKE

N/Réf. :

V/Réf. :

Objet : Transfert - de Malade
KATshini - Mulukai -

Cit : Médecin,

Je vous envoie l'enfant : KATshini - sexe : Masc. et
Agé : 6 ans.

Pour a 4 h.. du Matin au dispensaire avec
- Hyperthermie T: 40°C T. A 7/5
- Conscet : Respiration : néant.
. Battement cardiaque = Coeur : néant
. ne Réagit pas à l'injection
. Concl. Δ - Paludisme
- déshydratation

N.B. DéCéDé +

Voir hôpital M. M. yemo pour un certificat
de décès.

Assist. Médical Resp.
IWANGA - EMBUM.

Copy of the official Notification of Death from Mikondo Clinic verifying the examination of Katshinyi Manikai's body on June 12, 1985. Listed are the details of the examination and the concluding diagnosis: "deceased."

C.S.S.P.

C. A. D. Z.

Av. Kileyi No 10 Q. Mikon.'o
Zone de KIMBANSEKE

Kinshasa   June 12, 1985

N/Réf. :

V/Réf. :

Objet :   Transfer of Patient
Katshinyi Manikai

Dear Doctor,

I am sending to you this child, Katshinyi. - Sex: masculine.

Age: 6 years

Received at 4:00 O'clock in the morning with

- hyperthermia T 104°F B.P. 7/5

-Breathing : none

-Beating of heart: none

-no response to injection

-Malaria

-Dehydration

Note: DECEASED

See Mama Yemo hospital for death certificate

Medical Assistant in Charge
Iwanga Embum

The Notification of Death translated into English.

In the Cannon Room of the Congress of the United States of America in Washington, D.C, Mahesh leads the 1986 National Day of Prayer and Fasting, with Michigan Congressman Marc Siljander. This annual event is sponsored by Intercessors for America.

At a rally in Richmond, Virginia, Mahesh commissions black church leaders. Mahesh believes that the black church will play a prominent role in the revival that he believes will come soon to America.

Mahesh is interviewed on the air by host Scott Ross of CBN's "Straight Talk." His ministry has also been featured on the "700 Club."

ENCOUNTER WITH THE LORD OF EVIL

I shuddered as I recalled another terrifying incident when I knew I had come face to face with the work of the evil one. It had happened a few months before when I was working as assistant manager of a restaurant near campus. I was not baptized in the Spirit at the time and had very little awareness of the reality of the spirit realm.

Our chief cook, Ken, had asked if I could give a part-time job to his son, Tony, who was nineteen years old. I knew that Tony was a troubled young man. I also knew that his family was going through some hard times and that the extra income would mean a lot to them. I gave Tony a job as a busboy on the evening shift.

We began running into problems almost immediately. Tony often showed up late for work, and sometimes he didn't show up at all. His behavior was strange, too. He would be carrying a tray of dishes through the dining room and suddenly, for no apparent reason, he would lurch to the side and spill everything. I told Ken that if Tony's performance didn't improve, I was going to have no choice but to let him go.

One evening I came into the kitchen and found Tony wandering around the room, slashing the air with a huge kitchen knife. When I asked Tony what in the world he was doing, he looked at me with glassy eyes and said he was trying to get rid of some flies that were buzzing around the food.

That was too much. I grabbed Tony by the shoulders, put the knife away, and sat him down in an unused banquet room while I went to my office to call his father.

I hadn't even finished dialing the number when I heard one of the waitresses screaming, "Fire! Fire!" I ran to the banquet room. Tony had turned out all the lights and pushed the chairs and tables to one side. Then he had taken several cases of match boxes from a storage closet and was lighting them, several boxes at a time, in the middle of the floor. All the while, he kept chanting, "I must make a sacrifice. I must make a sacrifice. I must make a sacrifice."

I ran to the middle of the room and began stamping out the fire with my feet. Tony began to cackle in a weird, high-pitched voice I had never heard before. "You think you have power," he shrieked. "You have no power. All power is ours!"

Suddenly, I became uncomfortably aware of another presence in the room. I looked around in the dark, half-wondering who else might be there, half-afraid of finding out. Then I saw him: a dark, brooding figure looming in the corner of the darkened room. A sickening chill raced through my body. What was going on here?

By now the smell of the smoke and the shouts of the waitress had drawn the attention of the night-shift cook and one of the other busboys. The cook—a very large man—lunged at Tony, trying to tackle him like a football player. Tony just brushed him aside as though he had the strength of ten men. The other busboy and I just stood there, frozen with confusion and fear. All the while, Tony kept laughing and crying out nonsensically about "his lord" having "all the power."

His reference to his "lord" finally triggered something inside me. "*I have a Lord, too,*" I thought. "*If he's going to call on his lord, I might as well call on mine.*" I had never been in any situations like this before. I really didn't know what to say, and I was too scared to say anything out loud anyway, so I just prayed inwardly, "Lord Jesus, bless Tony. Bless him, Lord." Tony began to calm down somewhat. Slowly I edged closer to him. I was shaking like a leaf, I was so frightened. Every step I took in Tony's direction brought me one step closer to that terrifying... *thing* in the corner. I didn't dare to look at it, but I knew it was still there. I could just *feel* it.

Finally, I got close enough to Tony to reach out and place my hand on his forehead. "Lord Jesus, bless Tony..."

The instant my hand touched his forehead, Tony let out a piercing scream. "Stop it! Stop it!" he shrieked. "Get that cross off my head! It's burning me! It's burning me!"

"I'm not hurting you, Tony," I said. "It's just my hand." I kept praying. Tony slumped down into a chair. He let out a long, deep breath. It sounded like a tire releasing all its air. Then, he was still. I glanced toward the corner, where I had seen the mysterious, terrifying presence a few moments before. It was gone.

Soon Tony's father arrived and took him home. I later learned that Tony had been involved in some sort of satanic group. At the time, I didn't know what to make of that. I had never been taught anything about Satan and evil spirits. Still I knew that something very evil and very real had been in that room and had been at work in Tony.

JESUS CHRIST OVERCOMES THE EVIL ONE

Could that same something be at work now in Stevie?

I looked down at the bruised, bloody, calloused face resting against my chest. I pondered the words the Holy Spirit had spoken to me: *"This kind can come out only by prayer and fasting."* In the Gospel, this was a reference to an evil spirit. So the meaning seemed clear: Stevie's problem was caused by a demon. If I wanted to help him, I would have to deal with the work of that demon.

But how? In Tony's case, I had simply prayed that the Lord would bless him, and the demon left. I had been praying like that with Stevie for weeks now, but it had made no difference in his condition. I sensed that the answer lay in the word "fasting."

I had never been taught anything about fasting, but it

seemed clear to me that the Lord wanted me to do it, whatever it was. To me, to fast simply meant not to eat anything and not to drink anything: no food, no water, period. That's what I decided to do. I said, "Lord, if you want me to fast, I'll fast." I started that very day.

That first day went reasonably well. I was so excited at the prospect of what the Lord was going to do for Stevie that I didn't mind feeling hungry and thirsty. The second day was considerably harder. By the third day, I was really struggling.

I've since learned that it's not a good idea to go without water for an extended period. I didn't know that then, though, so I fasted even from water. On the second day of my fast, I was hungry, having visions of steaks and baked potatoes. By the third day, I was so thirsty that I didn't even think about how hungry I was!

I remember that day watching one of the other attendants wash his hands at the sink. The sound of all that water pouring out of the faucet and rushing down the drain—the very *idea* of all that water going to waste—was agonizing. I got angry and jealous. I still remember the startled expression on his face when I snapped, "What's the matter with you? Don't you know you could be drinking that?" Poor guy. He had no way of knowing what I was going through.

On the fourth day, I sensed the Lord telling me it was okay to drink water, but I continued fasting from food. Finally, after fourteen days, the Spirit said to me, "Now go and pray for Stevie."

I took Stevie into a small office that we sometimes used for staff meetings. He sat there, his arms fully extended to the sides, looking at me blankly.

"Stevie," I began, "I know you don't understand me. Your mind isn't capable of it, but your spirit is. I want to tell you that I am a servant of the Lord Jesus Christ. I've come to preach the good news to you, to tell you that Jesus came to set the captives free. God loves you, Stevie. He sent his Son, Jesus, to die for the sins of the whole world and to release us all from bondage to the devil."

Suddenly, I felt a tremendous surge of faith, a sense of authority and confidence. I looked at Stevie as though I were looking right into his spirit and said, "In the name of Jesus, you foul spirit of mutilation, come out of him *now!*"

As I said those words, Stevie's body was suddenly flung out of his chair and all the way back against the wall. It was like someone picking up a rag doll and tossing it across the room. He sat there on the floor for a moment, leaning back against the wall. Then, he opened his mouth and released a loud sigh. It sounded like a person who was choking, trying to exhale. It seemed to last for a full minute, this long, low sighing sound. For a moment, the room was filled with a smell like rotten eggs. Then, as suddenly as it had begun, the sighing stopped and the smell dissipated. Stevie just sat there on the floor, looking at me.

Something about him had changed. The whole room felt different. I untied his arms. Slowly, he raised his hands to his face. He began gently feeling his cheeks, his eyes, his mouth. Huge tears started to roll down his cheeks. I was crying, too. I realized that this was the first time Stevie had ever been able to touch his face without being driven to batter himself.

Over the next few weeks, Stevie's appearance began to change. The bruises and welts healed. The leathery skin turned soft and smooth. The swelling around his eyes and ears went away. Stevie never again had to wear his arm splints. From that day on, he never again exhibited the self-destructive behavior that had plagued him for so long. The Lord had delivered him.

My experience with Stevie taught me a great deal. It showed me how powerful evil spirits can be in bringing illness and heartache to human beings. It showed me how much more powerful is the name of Jesus to free us from their wicked purposes. It showed me the importance of fasting, which has played a vital role in my life and ministry ever since.

TEN

In the Holy Spirit's Secret Service

TRUSTING IN JESUS' HEALING LOVE

My time at the State School was my training ground for later ministry. I learned about the love of God and how it could triumph over sin and sickness and human misery. I learned about being attentive and obedient to the voice of the Holy Spirit. I learned about the work of Satan and evil spirits and about taking authority over them in the name of Jesus. I learned about the powerful spiritual weapon of fasting.

My supervisors at the school, obviously, were interested in seeing me make a difference in the lives of the children there. They were quite pleased with the good things they saw happening. I, of course, knew that it was not my skill as a member of the psychology task force that was making the difference. It was the love and power of God as I was able to communicate it through prayer and fasting.

Even though I kept working hard at my job, I also kept praying and fasting for different children as the Lord led me. I did this quietly and, for the most part, on my own time. It seemed to me that as long as I was an employee of the school, I was duty-bound to accept their standards and play according to their rules. I saw myself as a member of the Holy Spirit's "Secret Service." I didn't go around trumpeting what I was doing or taking credit for the results. When one of the children suddenly made an unexpected breakthrough in response to prayer, I rejoiced but said nothing. I knew that the Lord had done it, and the Lord knew it as well. That was enough.

Yet there was no mistaking the fact that there seemed to be a particular anointing at work when I prayed with people. I had never set out to be a "healer" or a "miracle worker." I had never asked the Lord for any particular ministry. I was not even an especially eloquent or dynamic pray-er. I would just ask the Lord to bless someone and reveal his love to them. When good things happened as a result—when someone was healed or released from bondage—I was just as surprised and fascinated by it as anyone else. I didn't know what to make of it, but there it was, just the same.

Occasionally, I would be specifically invited to pray with someone who was sick. One of the attendants at the State School knew about my prayer and fasting with the children. On one occasion, she asked me to go to Lubbock Methodist Hospital to pray for a young boy from the school who was near death. I later learned that the chaplain from the State School had already arranged for a casket to be sent to the school, because it appeared that this little boy might die at any moment.

I went to the hospital and was allowed to visit the boy's room. He was barely conscious. I prayed quietly for a moment and then began to share with him, in very simple terms, that Jesus loved him.

I talked for a few minutes. Then, for no particular reason, I leaned over and said, "Can you say, 'Jesus?'" No one had told me that he was mute and could not speak. Yet I asked him; and when I did, he looked up at me, smiled, and said the word, "Jesus." He was immediately healed. The chaplain had to send the casket back to the funeral home. They didn't need it any more.

In those days, there was a tremendous outpouring of the Holy Spirit all across the west Texas region. Prayer groups and home meetings were springing up everywhere. I began to participate in several of them and even became involved in leading them.

In fact, as my awareness of the healing and miracle-working power of God grew, I found myself seeking out every opportunity I could to be with people who were also experiencing the Holy Spirit. Almost every night that I wasn't on duty at the State School, I was in a living room or church basement somewhere, sharing about what the Lord was doing and trying to get to know him better. Some of the meetings were sponsored by Catholics and some by Protestants. I didn't care. I just wanted to be with people who loved Jesus.

Again, I never made a point of focusing on healing or on "my ministry." I would just share about the Lord's love. But people would get healed anyway. I started getting invited to different meetings to minister. I would come and speak briefly. I would usually just share about God's love, and God would be gracious and touch people.

About this time, a man I knew from one of the prayer meetings I attended, named Galen Carr, came to me with the story of a little boy named Drew Hall. Drew's parents were members of the local Methodist church where Galen was an elder. Drew had been born with a congenital heart defect that had required open-heart surgery. He was four years old. This kind of surgery on young children is fairly common today, but back then it was very new and very risky.

Drew was not expected to live. His parents had heard about me and had asked if I would be willing to pray for their son. The Halls didn't ask me to come and pray *with* him in person. They just wanted me to pray *for* him. Naturally, I told Galen I'd be more than glad to pray for this little boy, and I did, right on the spot.

As soon as I began to pray, I had a vision of the Lord. It wasn't just a mental image. My eyes were open and I saw him, just as I had seen him on the two previous occasions. This time he held a little child in his arms. As I watched, he gave a little gesture with his hand, as if he were signaling to someone. Somehow, in the context of the vision, I understood that he was signaling for music to begin.

Then, he began to dance. Holding the little boy close against his breast, he danced around and around, laughing merrily. I saw that the little boy was laughing, too. I could not hear the music, but I saw them dancing and laughing together for what seemed like several minutes. Then the vision ended.

I really didn't know what to make of what I had seen. Did the vision mean that the little boy would be healed? Or was it a picture of Jesus receiving him into heaven? I decided not to try to interpret it. I just told Galen what I had seen and asked him to relate the vision to Drew's parents. All this happened on a Tuesday.

On Friday of that week, Drew Hall died. I was greatly saddened by the news. My heart really went out to the parents. The Halls invited me to Drew's funeral. It was the first time I had met them. Despite their loss, they were radiant. They hugged me and said, "We just want you to know that your vision is what is sustaining us through this."

They invited me to their home the next week to meet some of their friends. They wanted me to tell them what I had seen when I prayed for Drew. I described the vision just as I had seen it.

Then the father got up. "I would like to share something with all of you," he said, "because Drew was born with a heart defect, he couldn't be like other children. He couldn't do the things they could do. All day long he would lie in his crib, waiting for his daddy to come home.

"When I would get home, I would put on his favorite music, pick him up from his crib, and dance all around the room with him. As I would dance, he would laugh and laugh. It was his favorite part of the day. Mine, too.

"I've never told Mahesh about this. But when he had his vision, we realized exactly what it meant. We knew that when Drew passed away, Jesus was going to take over right where we had left off. That's the only reason we've been able to come through this terrible ordeal the way we have."

There was not a dry eye in that room! I learned another important lesson from the Lord that night. When we pray for healing, we may not always get the answer we want. But we can always trust Jesus. We can release into his care the things that trouble us, because we know that his wisdom and love are infinitely superior to ours.

LETTING THE LORD LEAD

From time to time, I still experienced the Lord calling me to various particular situations. I never forgot that day at the State School, when the Spirit told me several times to "go back to Rose" and I almost dismissed his voice as my imagination. That had very nearly turned into a tragedy. Ever since then, I was fully committed to listening for the Lord's voice and to obeying him without question when he spoke to me.

So it was that one day, as I was going about my regular routine of work and classes, I heard the Lord speak to me. He said, *"Go to Dallas."* Not a very detailed set of instructions, but if the Lord wanted me to go to Dallas, then to Dallas I would go.

I only knew one person in Dallas. His name was Skip. I had met him in graduate school. His wife had left him and their two young sons—ages three and six—and he had had to leave school and move to Dallas to get a job. That was almost three years ago. I hadn't had any contact with him since then, but I still had his phone number. I called him up and said, "I'm going to be in Dallas for a couple of days. What do you say we get together?" He invited me to stay at his house.

I still didn't know why the Lord was sending me to Dallas. He hadn't given me any explanation or further instructions. He just said, *"Go to Dallas."* I knew my friend Skip wasn't a Christian. I knew he had been devastated when his wife left him and could only assume he was struggling to raise those children all by himself. I figured maybe the Lord wanted me to visit him so I could share my faith with him. So Thursday afternoon, after my classes were over, I walked downtown to the Lubbock bus station and bought a ticket to Dallas.

It was a frustrating weekend. Skip was trying to hold down two jobs to make ends meet and still be a father to his two boys. The house was total chaos. Skip was always exhausted. The two boys, on the other hand, never seemed to get tired. I kept waiting for an opportunity to talk to Skip about Jesus, but none presented itself. Evidently, the opportunity wasn't going to "just happen." I was going to have to *make* it happen.

No sooner had I decided I needed to do this than I ran into another obstacle, which was that the Lord wouldn't give me freedom to raise the topic. I would ask the Lord, "Shall I talk to him now?" The Lord would answer, *"No. Not now. Later."* All Friday night, all day Saturday and Saturday night, and all day Sunday this went on. I kept asking the Lord, "Now?," and he kept answering, *"Not yet."*

I was really getting frustrated. It was already Sunday afternoon, and I had to catch my bus back to Lubbock at seven o'clock Monday morning. When was I ever going to talk to Skip about Jesus? Why had the Lord dragged me off to Dallas for the weekend, anyway?

We had been invited to have Sunday dinner at the home of a couple who babysat for Skip's boys during the week. So we bundled up the boys and drove off across town to dinner. *"Great,"* I thought, *"Just great. I've been trying to share the gospel with this guy all weekend, and I haven't been able to get a word in edgewise even when we're at his house. How am I going to be able to talk to him at a dinner party at the babysitters' house?"* I was glumly expecting a dull evening of small talk with a bunch of strangers.

Was I ever wrong about that. As we pulled into the driveway, a woman—I could only assume it was our hostess—suddenly ran out the front door screaming, "He's killing my husband! He's killing my husband!" She was hysterical.

Skip and I raced into the house. We didn't see anyone there. For a moment, we couldn't figure out what was going on. All the while, the woman kept screaming, "You've got to stop him! He's killing my husband!" We ran to the kitchen in the back of the house.

Then we saw it.

In the backyard was a man. Again, I assumed it must be the husband. He was leaning against a tree, barely able to stay upright. His clothes were shredded and spattered with blood. One of his arms was slashed open from shoulder to elbow so badly that you could see the exposed bone. He was a frightful sight.

Even more frightful was the dog a few feet in front of him. A big dog. Probably the biggest German Shepherd I have ever seen, certainly the biggest I ever want to see. It was growling and snarling menacingly, crouched down as if on the verge of attacking again.

I tried to figure out what to do. I was in no hurry to mess with that dog. But the wife was continuing to cry and scream frantically, and it was clear the man wasn't going to survive another attack by that vicious dog.

In a split second, I made up my mind. I had to do something to help this man, to try to save his life. I rushed to the side door of the house. As I did, I noticed a broom leaning up against the wall. I grabbed it and headed for the back yard.

Just inside the fence was a patio with some folding lawn furniture arranged on it. I picked up one of the chairs. I must have been thinking of the lion-tamers I had seen in circuses. Maybe I could keep the dog at bay long enough for the man to escape. Slowly, I edged toward the dog, holding the broom and the chair out in front of me.

Suddenly, I heard the Holy Spirit speak to me: *"Bind it."*

"Bind it?" What did that mean? How did I go about "binding" something? What should I bind?

The words came again. *"Bind it!"*

The dog had now turned its attention toward me. I looked down at those crazed eyes, those ferocious teeth. Without really understanding what I was saying or why, I just stared back at the dog and said in a sharp, tense voice, "I bind you in the name of Jesus!"

Suddenly, a tremendous peace and calm came over me. All the fear just drained away. Something inside me seemed to sense that the danger was past now, that everything was under control.

The man was still slumped against the tree, just barely able to keep from falling over. I moved slowly, cautiously, in his direction, all the time watching the dog. The dog seemed different somehow. He was still snarling, still growling, still crouched as if to spring. But he seemed unable to move, as if his muscles had frozen. As if he wanted to jump but couldn't. As if he were ... *bound.*

Finally, I made it to the tree. I reached out to steady the man, and he simply fainted and collapsed in my arms. Apparently, the fear and the loss of blood were just too much for him. I tossed the broomstick over the fence, bent down, and hoisted him over my shoulder. I couldn't get back to the house without going past the dog, so I decided to just head for the fence. I used the chair to help me climb over into the neighbor's yard and lay the man down on the grass.

He was out cold and looked terribly pale. He had lost a great deal of blood, and the horrible gash in his arm was still bleeding. Someone brought me a towel, and with the towel and the broomstick, I made a tourniquet for his arm, to try to stop the bleeding.

I heard an ambulance pulling up in front. Apparently Skip or the wife or one of the neighbors had thought to call for it. Thanks be to God!

My moment of rejoicing was obliterated by a sudden flash of panic. I realized the man wasn't breathing! I put my hand on his chest, hoping to detect some slight rising and falling movement. Nothing. I grabbed his wrist and felt for a pulse. Nothing there either.

"O please, God," I prayed inwardly. "You can't let this happen. You just can't let him die." I was beginning to get a sneaking suspicion as to why the Lord had told me to come to Dallas. "I can't believe you brought me here just to see this man die."

The paramedics were coming through the gate now. I felt his chest again. Still nothing! I prayed earnestly. "O God, please."

Just then he let out a sigh. I was so happy, I almost fainted. As the paramedics lifted him onto the stretcher, he regained consciousness just for a moment. He opened his eyes and looked toward me. "Can this man come with us?" he asked the paramedics. "He just saved my life." Then he blacked out again.

Skip and I rode with him to the hospital. We paced around and around the waiting room until a doctor finally came and told us his friend would be alright. We collapsed into our chairs like a couple of limp dishrags.

We sat there for a moment in silence. Then Skip turned and looked at me. "That was amazing," he said. "Really amazing. I was so scared I couldn't do a thing, but you just walked out there as if you weren't afraid of anything—as if you weren't even afraid of dying. I've never met anyone with so much peace. What's your secret?"

At that moment, at long last, the Lord said to me, *"Now."*

I shared with Skip about the God who loved me, who loved him, who loved all of us so much that he sent his Son, Jesus, to die for us so that we could live forever. I told him that God wanted us to enjoy fellowship with him forever, but that our sins stood in the way. I told him that anyone who wanted could turn from their sin, welcome Jesus into their life as their Savior and Lord, and receive the gift of new life in his Holy Spirit. I told him that the moment they did this, they received not only the promise of eternal salvation, but also the promise of joy and of a peace that surpasses understanding even in this life.

I told Skip that if this was what he wanted, he could pray with me right then and there to receive Jesus into his heart. It was, and he did.

I might add that if this is what you want—joy and peace and life with God forever—you, too, can pray, right now, right where you are, the same prayer that Skip prayed that afternoon:

Lord Jesus Christ, I believe that you died for my sins, that you were buried, and that you rose again on the third day. I now repent of my sins and come to you for mercy and forgiveness. By faith in your promise, I receive you personally as my Savior and confess you as my Lord. Lord Jesus Christ, come into my heart, give me eternal life, and make me a child of God. Thank you. Amen.

It was that simple for Skip, and it's that simple for you, too. It's just that simple for everyone.

ELEVEN

Bonnie, My Wife, God's Choice

"He who finds a wife finds a good thing." Prv 31:10

CALLED TO THE PASTORATE

Since my canine adventure in Dallas, the Lord has brought me through a number of significant changes to put me on the pathway he has chosen. Shortly after that adventure, he told me that the time had come for me to put an end to my education. He also told me that my time of training at the State School for Retarded Children was over and that it was time for me to move on.

I can't say I was too upset to be done with graduate school. I had been spinning my wheels there for some time, even before I got baptized in the Spirit and began to pray for the sick. Since then it had become increasingly clear to me that, as interesting as my studies were and as much as I enjoyed them, they didn't represent the direction God wanted me to go. So when that semester ended, I just didn't register for the next one.

My feelings about leaving the State School were different. At first, I was heartbroken. I had been working there now for a year and a half. I had learned so much about the ways of the Spirit. I saw so many wonderful things happen in answer to my prayer and fasting. I loved those children so dearly. The thought of leaving them was more than I could bear.

Yet I had to admit that something needed to change in my life. I was living in my little shack, still working, still trying to fit occasional graduate school courses into my tight budget and even tighter schedule.

And I was increasingly involved in ministry. Every free night was taken up with visiting prayer groups and churches all around the area, giving my testimony, sharing the lessons I was learning about God's love, praying with people for healing from their illnesses and for deliverance from the work of evil spirits. One night I would drive thirty miles this direction, the next night I would drive fifty miles the other direction. The sessions often lasted into the early morning hours. There were times I would go for days on three or four hours of sleep per night.

One night, as I was driving home from yet another prayer meeting, the Lord asked me a rather unusual question. "Do you know how much you're earning for your labors?" he said.

I really had never thought about it in those terms. I didn't think of what I was doing as "labor" for which I ought to get paid. The groups I visited often took up some kind of offering for me. If I was lucky, these offerings would be enough to buy gas to get me home, but that was fine with me.

As I pondered the Lord's question, I thought, "Well, I suppose I could work out the math, but..."

I didn't need to work it out. The Lord did it for me. "You make about one-tenth of one cent per hour," he said. "That's not right. That's not the way I treat my servants." That was the first inkling I ever had that the Lord might want me to go into full-time ministry.

One of the groups I was most involved with was a prayer

group in Lubbock, where I worked closely with a man named Jim Croft. Jim, as it turned out, was to figure prominently in the future direction of my life.

I was also spending a lot of time with a group of people in Levelland. These were people who had come from a variety of churches and had been "invited to leave" their churches because they had gotten baptized in the Spirit. As time went on, they began to feel that they were to organize as a church, which they eventually did. In recognition of their varied backgrounds, they called themselves the Interfaith Church.

I had spent several weekends with them, sharing and teaching and ministering to people, and I liked them a lot. I was surprised when, one day, a group of them came to me and said, "We believe the Lord has spoken to us and told us you are to come and be our pastor."

"You do?" I said. "I mean, he has? Are you sure?"

"Yes," they replied. "We'd like you to move to Levelland and start right away. Will you do it?"

Being the pastor of a church was something that had never occurred to me. I didn't have a seminary degree. Being a professional clergyman had never appealed to me.

Still I had to admit that this invitation seemed to fit with everything else the Lord was doing in my life. He had told me to go to the State School as my training ground for ministry and now had told me that my time of training there was ended. I had grown to a point where I was confident about the anointing that the Lord had placed upon me for healing and deliverance. I had even been ordained an elder of the group in Lubbock where Jim Croft and I served together. Besides, I was twenty-nine years old, unmarried, with no particular career path before me, living in a hotel in Lubbock, Texas, and earning—by divine calculation—one-tenth of one cent per hour. Maybe it was time for something new.

I prayed about the invitation, and felt the Lord giving me leave to accept it. So in October of 1974, I became the first pastor of the Interfaith Church of Levelland, Texas.

Those were exciting times. In order to give adequate attention to my duties at Interfaith Church, I decided I needed to pull back from my activities and associations in many other groups. As I did so, many of the people from those groups began attending Interfaith Church in order to stay part of what the Lord had been doing among us.

There were people driving forty-five minutes, or an hour, or even more, to worship with us. They came from Lubbock, from Brownfield, from Amherst, from Sundown, from all over the region. They came Sunday morning, then came back Sunday evening, and then came back again for the Wednesday night prayer service. Our little church was growing rapidly not only in numbers, but also in love for one another and in the experience and exercise of the power of the Spirit.

We were especially blessed by the presence of a large contingent of young single people who were really hungry for the Lord and radically committed to being his disciples. They were incredibly zealous. Most of them had never experienced Christianity apart from a regular experience of the working of the Spirit. They thought that healings and deliverances were just an ordinary part of everyday Christian life.

MARRIAGE ANNOUNCEMENT FROM THE LORD

Bonnie Elkins was one of those singles. She had accepted the Lord at age eight. In high school, she excelled academically and became active in sports and cheerleading. Then, when she was sixteen, her parents got divorced. Immediately upon graduation, she took a summer job in upstate New York as a waitress in a resort. After that, she went to Dallas, found a job, and moved into her own apartment.

One day one of her co-workers asked her out of the blue if she knew whether she would go to heaven or hell when she died. Bonnie realized she didn't. Two days later she recommitted her life to the Lord. That very night back at her apartment, as she knelt by her bed to pray, the Lord baptized her in the Holy Spirit.

She was nineteen years old at the time—nine years my junior. She was the daughter of an influential rancher in western New Mexico. Bonnie had come to Lubbock to attend college and find a place to grow spiritually.

From the first, I saw that Bonnie was very much in love with Jesus and very sensitive to the Holy Spirit. She got acquainted with a number of the single brothers and sisters who lived in Lubbock and attended the church I was pastoring in Levelland.

It was especially encouraging to have Bonnie present when I ministered because she hung on every word, took extensive notes for personal study, and was outwardly responsive to what she heard. I still like to have her sitting where I can see her when I minister today.

Being still in my twenties, single, and pastor of a church with many singles in it, I was extremely careful about my social behavior, so as to never give anyone a reason to suspect my purity toward any woman. I looked upon the women in my congregation as my sisters in the Lord, first and only. In that context I had grown to appreciate Bonnie's presence during meetings. I had deep respect and trust for her ability to hear from the Lord through discernment and prophecy. On several occasions, the Lord had given her specific words of encouragement concerning my life and calling that proved very accurate.

So when she suddenly called me long distance from Lubbock one afternoon to tell me breathlessly of an unusual visitation she had had from the Lord, I didn't question it.

She told me how she had hurried home from school around five o'clock in the afternoon to spend some time in prayer and fellowship with the Lord, as she did every day at that time. As she lay on her bed, worshiping in the Spirit, she opened her eyes to see what appeared to be a mist slowly filling the room. She blinked her eyes several times and realized she was really seeing something supernatural.

With the thickening mist came the sense that she was before the very throne of the heavenly Father. "My first reaction," she said, "was to fall on my face before him. I was pretty scared, to say the least. Not because I was in trouble, but because God was showing up—in person!"

"What happened then?" I asked.

"Well, I just stayed there on the floor in the midst of this thrilling *presence*," she said. "It made me feel as though my body would burst. Yet it seemed that if it did it would only be more wonderful! After a time, I cautiously looked up. There in the doorway of my bedroom was the robed figure of a man. He was suspended about two feet off the floor. He appeared to be about thirteen feet tall, yet his whole figure fit between the floor and the ceiling! His face was shrouded by the mist, but when I looked at him, I immediately recognized in my spirit that it was Jesus.

"After a while," she said, "the mist began to roll away, just like it rolled in, and he was gone. I didn't move. I just kept my face to the carpet. Then, I heard his voice. It wasn't audible to my ears, but it was so clear within my spirit, it was unmistakable. This is the part that really got me stirred up. He said, 'You are going to be married soon.' Just like that, very calm. And that was it. He didn't say who, and he didn't say when!"

"Well, it sounds like you've had a visitation from the Lord alright," I said. "I guess we'll just have to wait and see about the when and the who."

It wasn't long before Bonnie began to get an inkling of who that individual might be. For days, even weeks, the Lord seemed to flood her mind with thoughts of marriage and family life, about being a godly wife and finding a godly husband. Every Scripture passage she read, every talk she heard, seemed to relate to this topic. In most cases, the Lord seemed to call her attention to the example of faith and godliness set by—her pastor!

She slowly began to realize that the Lord was no longer speaking to her about being married in the abstract, but very concretely about being married to *me*. She felt it was time to talk to someone other than me about all this. She chose Marie Middleton, the wife of one of the elders at Interfaith, and went to pay her a visit.

Marie, who had a knack for getting into unusual projects, was shelling a massive bowl of black walnuts when Bonnie arrived. She began the conversation by saying, "So, Bonnie, what's the Lord saying to you these days?"

Bonnie took a deep breath and said, "Well, actually, I think he's telling me I'm supposed to marry our pastor." There it was, out in the open.

Marie never even looked up from her walnuts. She simply and calmly replied, 'That sounds like the Lord to me."

In the meantime, I, too, was hearing from the Lord. After carefully guarding my heart against the possibility of any kind of romantic attraction to the young ladies in my church, I found myself inescapably drawn to Bonnie. My feelings became apparent to me when a young man in my church approached me as the pastor and expressed his serious interest in Bonnie. Instead of feeling like his pastor, I felt jealous.

Remarkably, in 1973, I had gone on a twenty-one day fast to ask God to find and prepare the bride he intended for me. I realized Bonnie's recommitment to the Lord and her move to Texas and to our Lubbock Bible group had coincided with this fast.

I took counsel with a number of men whose wisdom and maturity I respected, including my friend Jim Croft, who was now living in Fort Lauderdale, Florida. In fact, it was while I was in Fort Lauderdale, conducting a healing and miracle service, that I sensed the Lord giving me clear direction about the whole matter.

I took a long walk on the beach to sort out my feelings and get some guidance. As I was praying, I picked up some shells at my feet and was turning them over in my hand when I experienced the Lord in my mind's eye. He set Bonnie before me and said, *"This is the woman that I have given you."* I shared with Jim and some other men what I believed was the Lord's guidance. They affirmed that they felt I was hearing the Lord correctly.

When I got back to Texas I paid Bonnie a visit just to say "hello" and give her my souvenir shells from the beach, not mentioning the context in which I had collected them. Then I called all the elders of Interfaith Church together and asked for their discernment as well. Some of them, it turned out, had already heard from the Lord about Bonnie and me.

At this point, Bonnie and I had never even been on a date, let alone had a serious conversation about becoming husband and wife. Finally, in May, David and Marie Middleton invited us both to dinner and helped us get talking. We talked a long time—almost all night! I think it was about five o'clock in the morning when I proposed.

We set June 12 as our wedding date—less than a month away. We figured we had both heard from God, the elders and friends we looked to were in agreement, so why not get on with it?

Tragically for us and for our church family, a very dear brother in our fellowship, Earl Garner, passed away suddenly. Earl and his wife Ruby had adopted me a few years before as their spiritual son. Bonnie and I indefinitely postponed our wedding. Bonnie went to stay with Ruby for a while.

When we decided the time was right for us to resume our plans, I called my friend Jim Croft in Fort Lauderdale and asked him what might be a convenient date for him to come and perform the service. He glanced at his calendar and said, "Well, July 18 looks open."

And so it was on Sunday, July 18, 1976, that I married the woman God had chosen to be my wife. Like our "courtship" we had a rather unusual wedding. We held the Sunday morning service as usual, except this time Jim did the preaching and I took up the collection! Next Jim announced, "We are going to do something a little different this morning. Your pastor is going to get married." He stepped to the back of the church and escorted Bonnie to the front where I was waiting. Then turning us towards one another, Jim led us in pronouncing our vows.

It was all over in twenty minutes. I was soon to realize that in that short period of time, the best part of my life was beginning—and a new wind of spiritual direction was beginning to blow.

A Post-Graduate
Course in Healing

E VEN AS I SETTLED INTO MARRIED LIFE and resumed my duties
as pastor of Interfaith Church, my relationship with the
other leaders in Fort Lauderdale continued to grow stronger.
By December of 1976, our relationship had developed to
the point where they invited me to move to Fort Lauderdale
and join them. They believed the Lord wanted them to
start a local church in Fort Lauderdale and thought that my
gifts in healing and miracles would make an important
contribution.

I visited for a few days in January, and then went home
to take up the question with the elders of the church in
Levelland. They were sad to see me go, and I was sad to
leave. But we all agreed it was what the Lord wanted. So in
April, 1977, Bonnie and I moved to Fort Lauderdale to help
launch Good News Fellowship Church.

For the first year or so, I was primarily occupied with
pastoral duties in the local congregation. Bonnie and I hosted
a weekly gathering of thirty to thirty-five people in our home.
I would teach the Scriptures and pray for people as the Lord
led. I did a lot of counseling, helped plan the Sunday services,
helped train emerging leaders.

CALLED TO MORE THAN PASTORING

As time went on, the focus of my ministry began to shift. Even back in Texas, happy as I was working with a local congregation, I felt the Lord was giving me a burden for his broader purposes in the world. Reports of my miracle services were spreading and requests began to come in from all over the country for me to minister.

By the start of 1979, it was becoming clear that besides my local pastoral duties, God was calling me out on a wider scale to minister healing and deliverance. More and more requests were coming in—not just from cities in the United States, but from overseas as well. Everywhere we went, the anointing of God was powerful and unmistakable: healings, deliverances, miracles, conversions. It seemed we were poised on the edge of a major breakthrough into a more significant ministry.

Bonnie and I were to learn that there were more lessons the Lord wanted us to learn about his love and his power before we could take the next step in serving him. He taught us those lessons in a way that was both more painful and more glorious than anything we had ever experienced before.

On June 2, 1979, Bonnie gave birth to our first child, a boy. We named him Benjamin. I was a very proud father. All fathers are proud of their first-born children, of course, and most especially seem pleased if their first-born is a boy. For me it was even more significant. In my Indian tradition, a first-born son is considered a special blessing. As I held little Benjamin in my arms, I could feel rising within me the sense of dignity that came from being a *Rajput*, a "son of kings." Of course, what really made it special was the knowledge that both my little boy and I were beloved brothers of the King of kings, the Lord Jesus Christ.

In those first days, Bonnie and I went through the joys, anxieties, and confusions that are common to first-time parents. On the whole, everything seemed to be going well. We were proud and happy, and Benjamin was strong and healthy, or so it seemed.

On Monday mornings, the pastoral staff of Good News Fellowship would meet at the church for prayer. That's where I was, on a Monday morning about two weeks after Benjamin's arrival, when I got the phone call from Bonnie.

That morning she had taken Benjamin to the pediatrician for a routine check-up. At least, it was supposed to have been routine. As far as we could tell, Ben was perfectly normal. But the doctor evidently saw something that concerned him and ordered some special tests.

WOULD GOD HEAL OUR SON?

He was not encouraged by what he found. "I want you to go straight to the emergency room," he told Bonnie. "There appear to be two growths the size of lemons in his abdomen. We're not sure what they are, but we know they weren't there when he was born. We need to look into this right away."

I could hear the strain in Bonnie's voice as she recounted all this to me over the phone. "Just do what they say," I told her. "Get Ben over to the hospital quick. I'll meet you there."

As I rushed out the door, I called to the other pastors, "The doctors say there's something terribly wrong with our son. I've got to go to the emergency room right away. Please, pray for us."

It was about a thirty-minute drive to the hospital. I never knew thirty minutes could last so long. I was doing my best to pray, but I was greatly distracted by concern for my son. What could be wrong? Could it be a malignancy? But what kind of malignancy could grow so large so fast? My head was spinning. One moment everything was fine. The next moment it was anything but fine. I felt as though the whole world were crashing down around me.

When I finally arrived at University Hospital, the technicians were bringing Ben back from X-ray. The look on the doctor's face told me things were serious. "It's not tumors," he said. "It's worse. It's his kidneys. They're grossly enlarged and we don't know why." Ben would spend the night here, the doctor told me, and then be moved to Miami Children's Hospital in the morning. There were specialists there, he said, who might be able to do something.

He didn't sound very hopeful, neither did the specialists the next morning. Ben had a congenital defect, they explained, that made it impossible for his body to eliminate urine in the usual way. It was an extremely rare condition and a very serious one: 97 percent of all children born with it died within the first few weeks of life. Urine is one of the main ways that the body removes harmful waste materials. In Ben's case, those harmful materials were building up in his kidneys, and the toxins were being absorbed into his system.

The doctors felt that Ben needed an immediate operation to relieve the fluid build-up in his kidneys, but there was a problem. The very same fluid that threatened his kidneys had upset his blood chemistry so severely that his body could not possibly survive surgery. There was nothing to do, the doctors said, but "hope and pray" that his chemistry would change on its own so that they could operate.

For a couple of days, we did just that. The doctors hoped. Bonnie and I prayed, as did dozens of our friends and colleagues at the church. We prayed for Ben's healing. We prayed that his kidneys would return to normal. If nothing else, we prayed that his blood chemistry would become normal so the surgeons could operate.

Yet there was no change. The nurses would take a blood sample every thirty minutes and send it to the lab for testing. The key indicator was the level of potassium in the blood. If it went down, they could operate. It did not go down.

By Friday morning, Benjamin had gone into kidney failure. His skin had turned a ghastly blue-gray color, and his vital signs had all but disappeared. We could see that our son was dying. It was only a matter of hours.

All over the area, people were praying for Benjamin. The church had organized a number of emergency prayer meetings. Some of the home fellowship groups had conducted prayer vigils through the night. The other pastors, and many church members, were fasting.

It was all so confusing. I was regularly traveling across the country, and even to other countries, holding miracle services and seeing people instantly healed of serious, life-threatening illnesses by the power of prayer through the mere laying on of hands. Now here I was in this hospital with my own son on the verge of death. I had fasted. I had prayed. I had cried out to God. Still Benjamin slipped away, day by day, hour by hour.

I remembered the first lesson the Lord had taught me about his love and power, back at the Lubbock State School: never ask why. God's ways are beyond our ability to comprehend. Don't become bitter. Trust the Lord, no matter how agonizing the circumstances.

As I reflected on all this, on that heart-wrenching Friday morning, in a little alcove down the hall from Ben's hospital room, I knew what I had to do. I took Bonnie's hand and prayed what had to be the most difficult prayer of our lives.

"Lord, we love you," I said. "We belong to you. We are your servants. As much as we love our little Benjamin, we know that you love him even more." I was weeping so that I could hardly speak, but I knew had to press on. "Lord, we release our son to you. We want him to live. But we also want you to know that if you decide to take him, we won't take offense. We won't turn away from you. We won't ask why. We'll keep serving you and trusting in you. Amen."

I don't ever remember doing anything as difficult as praying that prayer. Perhaps no one who has not gone through the agony of losing a child can identify with what Bonnie and I felt at that moment, but we knew it was what we needed to do. We believed in healing. We had prayed for healing. Now it was time to let go and place Ben in the hands of the Lord.

We were still standing there in that little alcove, weeping, when the door burst open. It was one of the lab technicians. We looked up at him, expecting the worst. "You'd better hurry," he said. "It's Ben. His last blood test came back normal. They're taking him down to surgery right away."

The doctors never did offer an explanation of how Ben's potassium count could drop so suddenly and dramatically, but Bonnie and I already had all the explanation we needed. We knew the Lord was answering our prayers.

He kept on answering them. Over the next six months, Ben had to undergo five more operations. We practically lived at the hospital during that time. Bonnie slept there most nights, curled up on a couch in one of the waiting rooms.

Ben made steady improvement. Step by step, the doctors were trying to surgically reconstruct Ben's system so that he could urinate normally. In the meantime, they had implanted a complicated series of tubes that allowed the waste material to drain out through the side of his abdomen. He still was not healed. Tests showed that his kidneys were barely functional. Without healthy kidneys, Ben's prospects for a normal, fruitful life were greatly lessened. He was also far too young for the doctors to consider a kidney transplant.

His body did not always respond well to the surgery either. He would go through periods when his organs would try to reject the various tubes and other devices the surgeons had implanted. This was excruciatingly painful.

JESUS BEARS ALL OUR PAINS AND INFIRMITIES

As Ben lay in the intensive care unit following one of these operations, he was hooked up to monitors that showed when his body was spasming, reacting to the presence of the tubes. Every so often the needles on the monitors would lurch violently, showing that a spasm had begun. The doctors said that what Ben was experiencing was as intense as a woman's labor pains. Because pain medication would slow his heart rate, they could not prescribe anything to ease the spasms.

Ben would lie in his crib and scream with pain. Sometimes, he would thrash about so frantically that blood would ooze from his side, where the tube came out. It was almost more than I could take, to watch my child go through that kind of suffering.

"O God," I would pray at these moments, "you say in the Bible that your Son Jesus has come to bear all our pains and infirmities. Do that for Benjamin right now, Lord. Don't let him suffer. Bear his pains now, Lord Jesus."

We were allowed to sit with Ben for ten minutes every hour. When our ten minutes were up, we went back to the waiting room. During one of our hourly visits, the nurse glanced at the monitor and said, "Come and look. Something unusual is happening."

I looked at the monitor. The needle was all the way over, indicating that a spasm was underway. "I know," I said. "It looks like a bad one."

"No, not that," she said. "I mean, look at *him*."

I looked at Ben and saw that, despite the spasm, he was sleeping peacefully. There was even a smile on his face. His right hand was extended out in front of him, as though someone were holding it tight.

Tears came to my eyes as I watched. It was as though Jesus were reaching out to Ben, holding him by the hand, literally taking away his pain. Because Jesus is the eternal Son of God, and because Calvary is an eternal sacrifice, the Lord was able to reach down from the cross and take upon himself the very pain that Ben was suffering in that moment.

I sensed the Lord speak to me, deep in my heart. "Mahesh," he said, "do you know how you feel as you see your son in agony, with blood dripping from his side?"

I said, "Yes, sir."

The Lord said, "That's how I felt when I saw my Son hanging on the cross, with the blood flowing from the wound in his side. It is because my Son suffered in this way that your son need not suffer. This day I have healed your son."

It was true. Later the doctors ran a complete series of tests. They found that his kidneys were recovering. Regions in his urinary tract that had been non-functioning were now beginning to work normally. The hospital staff wasn't sure what to think. One of them suggested that perhaps their previous X-rays had been damaged, but Bonnie and I knew better. I had heard the Lord speak to me and knew he meant exactly what he had said. He was healing our son.

Six months after Ben was born, we took him home from the hospital. His kidneys began to regenerate, because of his age and because of God's miracle power. Today, as I write these words, Benjamin Chavda is a strong, healthy eleven-year-old boy. He has been totally healed from the affliction that almost took his life.

I was forever changed by the experience with Ben. I had prayed for healing for people many times in the past, but it would never be the same for me after that. Never would I be able to encounter someone who was sick without remembering the terrible anguish Bonnie and I had experienced. Never would I be able to minister to a sick person without identifying with the fear and confusion and heartache that were every bit as real to them as they had been to us. Never would I be able to pray for healing out of a selfish desire to impress people.

The Lord had taught me many things about healing during my years in Texas, but the experience with Ben was, for me, a sort of post-graduate course in healing. I would always carry in my heart the ache that I felt as I watched my son suffer, the ache that God the Father felt as he watched Jesus suffer, and the compassion with which he looks upon all his children who are afflicted. Because of the pain I had carried in my heart for Ben, I would always have room in my heart for the pain of others.

The Sorcerer's Tree

A FTER BEN'S HEALING, the pace of God's action in our life picked up markedly. I still had pastoral responsibilities in Good News Fellowship Church in Fort Lauderdale. But more and more, the Lord seemed to be shifting my ministry emphasis to healing, miracles, and evangelism.

Whenever I shared about the love of God, his power was there to confirm the message with signs and wonders. As a result, the scope of my ministry grew in the United States and overseas. I conducted evangelistic campaigns, leadership seminars, and healing services all over the world: I visited Russia, Yugoslavia, and Czechoslovakia; Egypt and Israel; and many countries in Europe, Africa, and Latin America. My primary focus, however, has been Africa: especially Zaire, Zambia, the Ivory Coast, Cameroons, and South Africa. Every year I have participated in a major gathering called the International Christian Celebration, held in Jerusalem during the Feast of Tabernacles.

Three main threads have run through my ministry. The first is the Great Commission: Jesus' command to all his followers to "Go into all the world and make disciples." The second is empathy for the pain of others. I've often told people that through the months of working with retarded children and through the harrowing experiences Bonnie and I had with Benjamin, God broke off a little piece of his heart and put it in me. Feeling the hurts of others drove me to reach out to them. The third is the supernatural. Ever since the Lord told me to pray for my mother and her miraculous healing, I've continued to trust God to intervene powerfully in people's lives. And he has.

THE POWER OF PRAYER AND FASTING

Never underestimate the power of prayer and fasting; it has been the undergirding of my ministry. For instance, during my fasts, it is not uncommon for God to give me special words of revelation and insight into his mind—sometimes about situations that have stumped me.

I will never forget the puzzling and embarrassing case of a seventy-year-old woman who was blind and received prayer for healing seven times! It was during a week-long campaign in 1986 to the Island of Haiti—a country where many are in bondage to the demonic forces of voodoo.

The evening rallies were held in an open field outside the city of Carrefoure, population seven hundred thousand, five miles from the outskirts of Port-au-Prince. Every night I would preach the gospel and then pray for the sick.

The very first night this seventy-year-old woman who was blind came forward for prayer, convinced that God was going to heal her. I laid hands on her and rebuked the spirit of blindness.

The power of God came over her, and she was slain in the Spirit. A few moments later she was helped to her feet, and I asked her, "Can you see?"

"No," she replied. With that, she was led back into the crowd, so my team and I could pray with others.

This happened every night for six days. She was always the first person in line to request prayer for healing. Every night I would lay hands on her and rebuke the spirit of blindness; then she would be slain in the Spirit. After she had gotten to her feet, I would ask again, "Can you see?"

She would reply, "No," and then disappear into the crowd every bit as blind as before.

After six nights of this, you can imagine my reaction when I saw her in line again on the seventh and last night of the campaign. I thought I would lay hands on her more out of compassion for her unrelenting faith than for any other reason.

Once again, she was slain in the Spirit after I prayed for her. After she was helped to her feet, I asked yet another time, "Can you see?"

Imagine my great joy when this seventy-year-old woman of faith turned to me, her eyes flashing, and said, "I can see clearly. Hallelujah!"

But I remained puzzled. "Lord," I asked on the plane flight back home after the campaign, "why did it take six times with no apparent results, and then all of a sudden she was healed?"

I didn't get my answer until my next forty-day fast. "Remember the woman in Haiti who was healed of blindness after seven nights of receiving prayer?" he asked.

"Yes," I replied.

"Her blindness was being held in place by demonic powers that were similar to an octopus. Each night as you prayed, an arm of the octopus would let go. But it was not until the last tentacle was pulled off that she was able to receive her sight.

"Sometimes prayer for healing happens like that. So it is your job to be faithful to pray, it is my job to heal according to my word."

Ever since I read about fasting in the Bible, I've practiced it in my own life and experienced its fruit, especially with regard to deliverance.

For many years now, I have made it a regular practice to go on two forty-day fasts each year, in January and August, as well as two twenty-one-day fasts. That kind of regimen is not for everyone, I know. But I feel certain it is what the Lord has called *me* to do.

It hasn't always been easy. Once in Texas I was on the nineteenth day of a forty-day fast when a bag of potato chips in the cupboard began to attract my attention. They almost seemed to be speaking to me: "Eat us, Mahesh. Don't leave us sitting here, salty and chewy and all alone. Eat us!" I guess my heart of compassion for those potato chips got the better of me. I ripped that bag open and devoured every last chip. Then I sat down, licked my fingers, repented, and resumed my fast—which I finished without further incident.

Often as a time of fasting approached, the Lord would give me a special prayer assignment for that fast. He might call me to pray for an individual or a church or a city. In time, he would call me to intercede and do spiritual warfare on behalf of whole nations.

Once he told me to use my prayer and fasting to combat the disease of cancer. In the months that followed, I experienced greater success in praying for cancer patients than I had ever known.

One man in particular stands out in my memory. His first name was Tony. I first met him in 1988, when I was ministering in Chicago. Tony was literally carried onto the stage by four men. His body was utterly wasted by lymphatic cancer and cancer of the bone marrow; all his hair had fallen out. His pastor told me the doctors estimated that Tony had less than a month to live. I had no trouble believing it.

I prayed and laid hands on him. It was as though the power of God came and knocked him over backward. He said he felt strength come into him, but he didn't look any different.

A year later, I went back to Chicago. I was introduced to a tall, healthy man who gave me a handshake that almost tore my arm off. It was Tony. He had been completely healed!

In learning about healing, deliverance, fasting, and prayer, I read the descriptions of what Jesus did while he walked the earth. I figured that if Jesus really was, as Scripture says, "the same yesterday and today and forever" (Heb 13:8), then these works should still be available to us today. My experience has shown that they are.

Thus, my ministry always proceeds, first and foremost, from the Bible. The more I visit the incredibly diverse cultures of our world, the more I realize how truly universal the Bible's message is. If we truly preach the gospel of Jesus, we never have to change our message when we cross cultural lines.

HOW GOD HAS LED ME IN MINISTRY

I always make sure that the people who come to my meetings hear a clear, simple presentation of the gospel message and have an opportunity to commit their lives to Christ. We have calculated that more than half a million people have come to a saving knowledge of Jesus Christ through our ministry over the years.

Most of our ministry is to the poor, though I have seen people from all walks of life respond to the gospel. Even people in the most powerful governmental positions have humbled themselves and submitted to the gospel of Christ as they have seen the healings and miracles that testify to its power.

Whenever possible, we invite the new converts to be baptized in water. I remember one time in Zaire I had the privilege of joining with about thirty-five local pastors in baptizing some three thousand new converts in a river. It was one of the highlights of my life.

It was also one of the scariest moments of my life. Because the river we were using was on an international border, we were accompanied by a platoon of soldiers. All of a sudden, the soldiers began firing their automatic rifles into the river, no more than a few feet from where we were conducting the baptisms. I looked up to see why they were shooting. I could see nothing but a few logs floating down the river.

Then it dawned on me: those weren't logs. Those were *crocodiles!* If I hadn't been up to my knees in sticky mud, I would have jumped out of that river in a single bound. Thank God, no one was hurt, either by the gunfire or by the crocodiles.

My usual pattern during a campaign is to preach a series of open-air evangelistic meetings in the evenings and give systematic teaching from Scripture on the foundations of faith and of Christian living during the days. I will minister healing and deliverance at all these sessions, asking the Lord to confirm the truth of his message by works of power. Sometimes I will set aside entire days for nothing but prayer ministry. Once in Kinshasa, Zaire, I laid hands on more than fifteen thousand people in a single day.

I work as closely as possible with the pastors in the area, because I want the lasting fruit of my ministry to be seen in strengthened local churches. Often this includes the launching of new churches. A denominational leader once told me, "Mahesh, when you first came to Kinshasa in 1985, we had four churches. Because of the converts that have been added through your campaigns and the training you have provided for our leaders, we now have more than one hundred churches in Kinshasa alone."

As a rule, all expenses for our campaigns are underwritten by our ministry organization. Even so, I encourage the collection of an offering at public meetings because it gives every person an opportunity to share in the work of the kingdom. These monies are then used to defray expenses of the campaign itself or distributed for the ministry of the gospel in other ways in that area.

Once when I was ministering in Africa, the Lord gave me an inner vision of two men and told me they had been stealing from the offerings. He said to me, "I want you to warn these men that if they do not repent, the angel of death is going to visit them before the night is over."

That's not the kind of message I am usually called to proclaim. Proclaim it I did, however. Within a few minutes, two men came forward and admitted that they had indeed taken money from the offerings for their own personal use. There were more than one hundred thousand people in the audience at the time, and they went home convinced that God really does know the heart and actions of every single one of us!

The manifestation of the supernatural power of God is a key element of my ministry, especially in the Third World. I regularly lead people in prayer to be baptized in the Holy Spirit and have seen the Lord touch as many as thirty thousand people at a time in this way.

Sometimes we see what I call "the firestorm of the Spirit." In a forest fire, the heat can become so intense that entire sections of trees simply explode into flames all at once. In the same way, in a meeting, the anointing of the Spirit can become so intense that whole crowds of people are simultaneously overwhelmed by the presence and power of God. The Spirit seems to come upon them in mighty waves.

When this happens, it doesn't seem to matter what I preach about, or how I try to conduct the meeting. The Lord just takes over. I've seen whole sections of people on cots and stretchers suddenly be touched by the Spirit's power, rise to their feet, and start dancing with joy.

THE STRONGHOLDS OF SATAN ARE DESTROYED

In my work in Africa, I have found that many regions are under the domination of sorcery and witchcraft. Masses of Africans live in mortal fear of the local witch doctors. This is not without reason: these witch doctors wield terrifying spiritual power to bring sickness, calamity, and death upon the people. I often teach special seminars to the pastors about the power and authority we have, in Jesus' name, over the works of darkness.

Confrontations with sorcerers and witch doctors are not uncommon at our meetings. Once in the Kananga province of Zaire—a region known for being a center of sorcery and witchcraft—I had an especially interesting incident.

It was in the city of Mbujimai. I was ministering healing. There were several hundred people gathered together to receive prayer. One of them, though I did not know it at the time, was the chief sorcerer of the city. He had been hired by witch doctors in the region to come to the meeting and place a curse on me.

I moved through the crowd, praying over people. All the while I was coming closer to this sorcerer, though I did not realize that was what he was. Finally, I reached the place where he was standing, and I reached out to place my hands on him. As I did, I suddenly heard this strange noise coming from him. It sounded like several animals all crying out at once. I looked up at his face. He was a very tall man. His eyes were completely rolled back into his head, so that all I could see were the whites of his eyes.

The only discernment I had at that moment was to think, "This man has a problem." The only thing I could think of to say was, "Bless him, Lord."

As I did so, it was as though two thousand volts of electricity jolted his body. He was flung through the air like a rag doll and landed with a thud about ten feet away. I mean, he hit the ground *hard*. I thought, "Lord! Be gentle!"

I went over to see how he was doing. He was trying to get up, but he couldn't. He squirmed and twisted and struggled, but he couldn't get up. It was as though an invisible angel were sitting on him.

I went on to pray for others. Sometime later, I came back to get a drink of water and found this man standing with the pastors. It was only then that I learned who he really was and what had happened to him. He had been unable to get up from the ground, he told the pastors, until he acknowledged Jesus Christ as Lord.

When he saw me, his eyes grew as large as saucers, and he started to tremble. He pointed at me and said, "The spirit that is over this man is greater than any spirit I have ever seen." Now this was a man who had seen quite a few spirits in his day, but he had never seen anything like the Spirit of our God!

At the end of the campaign in Kananga province, I told the people that they no longer needed to fear the power of the witch doctors, because a far greater power was available to them in the name of Jesus. I led them in prayer, renouncing sorcery and witchcraft, and pulling down Satan's stronghold in the region.

Next morning a messenger arrived at my hotel room. "Something remarkable has happened," he said. "The Sorcerer's Tree has been burned to the ground. You must come at once and see." I was just getting ready to leave for the airport, and I have learned never to take chances with air connections in central Africa, so I said, "I'm sorry, but I simply have no time."

By the time I returned to Zaire a year later, the story of the Sorcerer's Tree had become a local legend. Three years later I was able to see for myself the dramatic evidence of what God had done.

It seems that on the last night of the Kananga campaign, while I led the people in prayer against the powers of evil, a group of witch doctors had gathered at a spot about seven miles from where we were meeting. It was marked by an enormous tree known throughout the area as the Sorcerer's Tree. They were there to call down curses upon our meetings and upon various individuals. According to one of them, who later came to Christ, they were even discussing whose flesh they were going to eat.

Suddenly, as they were talking and as we were praying, they saw fire streak across the heavens. It seemed to be coming from the general direction of our meeting. It shot across the night sky and fell upon the Sorcerer's Tree. The leaves and branches were consumed, leaving nothing behind except the charred trunk.

That tree stands to this day outside Kananga. It had once been more than thirty feet tall. Now it looks like the remains of a huge match stick, burned from the top down. The trunk is not split, as it likely would have been had it been struck by lightning. The first several feet of the trunk are untouched, which would not be the case if someone standing on the ground had set the fire. I have spoken with several people from the village who saw the fire come from heaven and consume the tree from the top down. They also testify that three of the witch doctors died later as a result of the fire.

It was quite a moving experience for me to see the Sorcerer's Tree. As I walked up to it to touch its bark, I remembered Elisha's question, "Where now is the LORD, the God of Elijah?" (2 Kgs 2:14). I thought to myself, *He is here. He is among us. He is with us in power and might. He is here by his Spirit to glorify his Son, Jesus, by doing the same works through his servants today that he did through Jesus—even to the raising of the dead.*

FOURTEEN

The Resurrection of Katshinyi

"The Lord is showing me that there is a man here whose son died this morning. If you will come forward and receive prayer, God wants to do something wonderful for you."

THE FIRST TIME I HAD GONE BACK to Africa was in 1984. It was the first time I had been there since coming to the United States as a student, so many years before. Somewhere deep inside, I had always assumed that someday the Lord would bring me back to the land of my birth. But I had never sought for it, never pressed the Lord to bring it about. I simply assumed that when the right time came, he would make it clear to me.

On my first trip, I accompanied my friend and colleague Derek Prince, a noted Bible teacher. We ministered together in a number of locations across the country of Zambia. It was there that I was summoned late one night to a village in the bush country where a little boy had died of cerebral malaria. I prayed that he might be restored to life, but nothing happened. As I stood outside his family's hut, with the African wind swirling around me, I heard the voice of the Holy Spirit: *"Because you have been faithful,"* the Lord said, *"I will let you see great things."*

A SPECIAL INVITATION

Now, in 1985, I was going back. Again I was to travel with Derek. Again we were going primarily to Zambia. I, however, was making a side trip to Zaire, in answer to an invitation that had come in the mail the previous January.

The invitation itself arrived written on yellowed stationary, typed on an old manual typewriter with a couple of letters missing. The writer introduced himself as a pastor from Zaire to whom I had ministered during a healing session at the Feast of Tabernacles Celebration in Jerusalem.

He wrote, "With me was also another brother from Zaire who was suffering for many years with a serious back condition. When you prayed for him, he was put to the floor in the power of the Spirit; and when he stood again he was completely healed. Glory to God! The Lord has shown us that if you will come to Zaire and minister to our people, our nation will be changed forever." It was signed Pastor M'Poy M'wambi.

I hesitated. Change their nation forever? Who were these guys? I could not remember them from Jerusalem—there were always so many people who came for healing. The appearance of the invitation made me wonder how they would ever be able to arrange the meetings if they didn't even have a typewriter that had all the letters!

Yet their request stayed in my mind. I struggled with it. Should I go halfway around the world to a place and people I knew nothing about? I wasn't hearing God's answer about what to do.

I was discussing the situation with Jim Croft and he asked, "How much will it cost?" That was it! Surely the plane ticket alone would cost far more than our small budget could handle. I would have my secretary check the prices. Then I would write and tell them that it was financially impractical for me at this time, but I would consider their request at a later date.

When I got the information back, I had to look twice. The

entire extra leg of the journey—from Zambia, where I would be with Derek, to Zaire and back—would cost a total of twenty-seven dollars! I had never flown anywhere before—and I have never flown anywhere since—for only twenty-seven dollars.

We were scheduled to leave for our two-month journey at the end of May. But at the beginning of May a complication arose, a serious complication.

A SECOND SON, A SECOND TRIAL

In February, we learned that Bonnie was expecting our fourth child in September. Our daughters, Anna and Serah, had been born without mishap in the four years since Ben's birth. Once we got through Ben's ordeal, we figured that we had suffered our fair share of trauma over a child's health.

We were wrong.

Within days after discovering she was expecting, Bonnie began to hemorrhage. The doctors said she had a severe case of something called "placenta previa centralis." The placenta was under great stress, they said, and the pregnancy was in danger.

We were told that even a slight hope of delivering a live child would depend on her complete bed rest for the duration of the pregnancy. So Bonnie went to bed and I became Mr. Mom.

I had prayed for thousands of people to be healed before, and I thought I knew what it meant to pray earnestly. However, I can assure you I have never prayed for anyone as earnestly as I prayed for Bonnie. I have to admit that my motives were somewhat selfish. Until she got strong enough to get out of bed, I had to care for our three small children all by myself! Thank God for the assistance of our "adopted grandmother," Lois Hanks, a woman from our church whom we call "Yoo-Hoo."

By April things looked grim. Our obstetrician informed

us that there was only a 25 percent chance of the baby being carried long enough to deliver. Even then, there was no telling what complications might be present. His primary concern was for Bonnie because of the dangers of hemorrhaging. A slight crisis could easily create a situation in which he could not replace her blood loss quickly enough to save her life. Still he respected our commitment to do everything possible to save the baby.

We took it one day at a time. Bonnie would have occasional spells of premature labor. During one of these, half of the battered placenta broke off and fell out. At such times we would grit our teeth and pray. On more than one occasion, we decided that a little comic relief would be welcome. I would join Bonnie on the bed, and we would listen to Bill Cosby tapes and laugh.

On April 27, Bonnie went into labor for real. She was barely twenty-four weeks pregnant. She was rushed to the hospital and given medication to stop the contractions—but was also prepped for a premature delivery. Then miraculously, the labor stopped. We looked at our doctor, he looked at us— there was nothing to do but wait it out. For the next week none of us slept much. It seemed as though we were nearing the last marker in a marathon race for the life of our child. Bonnie was approaching twenty-five weeks. Every day gave the baby a better chance.

On May 5, Aaron Chavda was born. He weighed one pound eight ounces. I remember looking at him in the incubator and thinking in wonderment, "This is my son." He was the tiniest human being I had ever seen. His first sounds were three little "mews," like those of a tiny newborn kitten, as he was rushed to intensive care in the neonatal unit.

Our obstetrician, whose long vigil with us was now coming to an end as a new team of specialists took over, looked at us and said, "I have never seen anyone closer to God."

The next few days revealed that Aaron had a number of severe complications. They included blood in his spinal fluid, which doctors felt was an indication of cerebral hemorrhaging and possible brain damage, and a complete intestinal block caused by a length of his intestine having been dead for some time, giving way to toxic peritonitis. This condition gave reason to suspect the presence of cystic fibrosis or some related congenital disease.

Bonnie and I stared at each other in disbelief. Here we were again! The memories of Ben's ordeal came flooding back. Yet even though we had shared this kind of pain before, this new situation came with its own set of fears. We were walking this path, with *this* son, for the first time. Once again, only the Son of God knew where it would take us.

A PAINFUL DECISION

I was scheduled to leave for Africa the next week. I agonized over what to do. The plans for the trip were so complex that there was no way to change them. I didn't want to drop out of a ministry trip that I felt the Lord had so clearly called me to take. I did not want to disappoint the people who would be waiting for me. But I also didn't want to leave Bonnie at such a vulnerable time. It seemed clear that unless the Lord intervened in a most dramatic fashion, Aaron had only a few more days to live. If I left, Bonnie would have to bury him alone.

In the end, we decided I should go to Africa as planned. I have never made a more difficult decision. I never *could* have made it without Bonnie. "Your job is to go where the Lord has called you to go," she told me. "After what we went through with Ben, I know that what matters isn't whether or not you're here, but whether the Lord is here. And I know he is here. If Aaron lives, it will be because God intervenes, not because you're home."

I spent a few minutes alone with Aaron before I left. I anointed him with oil and prayed over him. Then I said, "Aaron, it looks as though I may not see you again. I want you to know that your daddy loves you. But Jesus loves you even more than I do. If I never see you again here on this earth, I know I'll see you in heaven." Then I left for the airport.

Our time in Africa was powerfully anointed from the start. We saw healings, deliverances, conversions. Still Bonnie and Aaron were never far from my thoughts. I was able to reach Bonnie by phone once, from Zambia. I was overjoyed to hear that Aaron was still clinging to life. The next day, I caught my plane to Zaire.

That week in Kinshasa was unlike anything I had ever experienced before. I found myself caught up in a major visitation of the Holy Spirit. The family of the country's president attended the campaign. The leading general of the army and the head of the civil services were converted and filled with the Holy Spirit. So many sick people came seeking healing, that one day I did nothing from nine in the morning until six in the evening but stand and lay hands on people as the whole long line of them filed past. It was estimated that we prayed for more than fifteen thousand people on that day alone.

The next day, I had a one-hour break before the evening session, and I left strict instructions with the hotel not to disturb me under any circumstances. I just wanted to put my feet up for a few minutes and catch my breath. I had scarcely lain down when there was a knock at the door. It was a man from the hotel staff. He was terribly sorry to disturb me, he said, but there was a group of men in the lobby who insisted they had to see me. Wearily, I dragged myself to the lobby. There I found twenty-five members of the country's parliament, on their knees, asking if I would lay hands on them and bless them.

By far the most memorable moment of the trip came on

Wednesday morning, when I spoke to a crowd of thirty thousand people in Kinshasa's Kasavubu Square. I had just finished my talk and stepped back from the microphone when the Holy Spirit spoke to me. *"There is a man here whose son died this morning,"* he said. *"Invite him to come forward and receive prayer. I want to do something wonderful for him."*

I felt a sudden stab of pain in my heart as I heard the Lord say these words. I thought of my own son, Aaron, lying in that intensive care ward back in America. For all I knew, the man whose son had died that morning might be *me.*

I obeyed. I stepped back to the microphone and said what the Lord had told me to say. Almost immediately, a man came running from the back of the crowd, waving his hand in the air and shouting, "It is I! It is I!" I placed my hands on his shoulders and prayed for his son. Then I watched as he went running from the square.

THE STORY OF KATSHINYI

Mulamba Manikai lived with his wife and son on Lumbi Street, in the Mikondo section of Kinshasa. Unlike most of their neighbors, and most of their family, they were Christians. When Mulamba heard there would be meetings in downtown Kinshasa at which a man from America would be preaching the Word of God, he arranged his work schedule so he could attend. Though I did not know it at the time, he was one of the two thousand people who had attended our first session on Monday morning.

When he returned home that day, he was distressed to learn that his six-year-old son, Katshinyi, had fallen gravely ill. Mulamba tells what happened next:

"When I got home from the meeting, I found my son paralyzed. He could not eat, could not stand, could not sit. When I touched his body, his skin felt hot.

"My wife had called my older brother, Kuamba. He was

angry with me. Your child is sick. How can you put this business of God ahead of your child?'

"On Tuesday, my brother and I took the child to the dispensary of the company where I worked. They ran tests. They told us he had cerebral malaria. It was very bad. They told us to go the next day to the clinic in Mikondo and they would give us medicine.

"We had to get up very early on Wednesday to get to the Mikondo Clinic. I was very worried. It was more than twenty-four hours now, and my son had not spoken. He had not moved. As we came close to the clinic, my son suddenly arched his back and threw back his head. Then he went all limp. He did not breathe. His heart did not beat. He had died in my arms. This was about four o'clock in the morning.

"The doctor at the clinic gave my son an injection to revive him. It did nothing. He stuck needles into his arms and his chest. My son did not respond. He lit a flame and held it against my son's legs. Still he did not respond. Finally, he told me, 'Your son is dead. I can do nothing for him. You must take him to Mama Yemo Hospital in Kinshasa and get a death certificate to bury him.'

"At the hospital, they took one look at my son and said, 'He is dead.' I said, 'Is there nothing you can do?' They said, 'You must go and buy a burial permit for your son's body.'

"But I had no money. So I left my son's body at the hospital, with my brother. I went to the company where I worked, to see if I could borrow some money. As I stepped into the street, I prayed, 'You are the great God. If it gives you glory for Katshinyi to die, then let him die. But if not, then let him live again. I have told many people that you are the Good Shepherd. How will they believe me if my own son dies?'

"I remembered the story in the Bible where the woman Dorcas dies. Peter, the servant of the Lord, has just arrived in her city. He prays for her and she comes back to life. The Lord spoke to me then. He said, 'Why are you weeping? My servant is in this city. Go to him.'

"I went to Kasavubu Square, where I had heard Mahesh preach before. As I arrived, he stepped back from the microphone. I was sad because I thought he was done praying for people. Then he went back to the microphone. He said, 'The Lord has shown me that there is a man here whose son has died this morning. Come forward and the Lord will do something wonderful.'

"I went running to the front. Mahesh prayed for me. I felt great joy. I felt faith inside me. I knew God would answer these prayers. I ran back to the hospital right away."

During the time Mulamba was gone, his older brother Kuamba stayed with Katshinyi's body at the hospital. He describes what happened:

"We were left alone. We were crying. Many people were gathered around us, and we were crying. The nurses told us to just go back home as this child had already died.

"It was midday. I was sitting there holding the body of my brother's son in my arms. Suddenly, I felt his body move. Then he sneezed. He sat up in my arms and asked for something to eat. He began to say, 'Where is my father? Where is my father?'

"At that time his father came back. When he found the child crying, 'Where is my father?' he was so joyful. He told us how he had gone to the campaign and heard the man say to come forward. All of the people in the hospital, including the nurses, were amazed. My brother was praising God in a loud voice. Many people thought he was mad because he was shouting. He said, 'God is good. He is true. My tears have turned into joy.'

"The following day we went to the campaign. We went to see face-to-face the man who had told of this miracle. We saw the blind recovering their sight. We saw the lame put away their crutches. When we saw these things, we said that God is good. All of our family has repented. We have believed in the Lord Jesus Christ."

"I WILL LET YOU SEE GREAT THINGS"

A couple weeks later, I returned to Fort Lauderdale. My first question when I was picked up at the airport was, "How is Aaron?" Imagine my delight to hear that he was still alive! He had survived the operation. It had been a struggle, but he had hung onto life all these weeks, daily growing in health and strength. Today, as I write these words, Aaron is a bright, vigorous, five-year-old boy. The Lord has healed him completely.

I have been back to Kinshasa several times since that first visit in 1985. Our team has spent extended time with Mulamba and his brother. We have talked with pastors in the area and also with doctors and nurses at the Mikondo Clinic and Mama Yemo Hospital. They have verified the story of Katshinyi's sickness, his death, and his return to life.

We have also spent time with Katshinyi and his family. They still live at 26 Lumbi Street in Kinshasa's Mikondo section. Mulamba's brother, Kuamba, and all the other members of their families, still faithfully follow the Lord Jesus. They still tell friends, co-workers, and neighbors about the great thing God did for them. Mulamba and Kuamba have started a Bible study and prayer group, as well as a children's choir numbering seventy-five children.

Katshinyi is a remarkably normal little boy. He only vaguely remembers the details of what happened to him on that extraordinary day in 1985. His feet and legs still bear the scars where doctors at the Mikondo Clinic burned him with an open flame, to satisfy themselves that he was indeed dead.

On Sunday, the last day of that momentous 1985 campaign, Mulamba came forward to share publicly for the first time about the great thing God had done for his son. A million thoughts were racing through my mind. I thought of the hundreds of people who had been touched by the healing power of God that week. I thought of the thousands who had given their lives to Jesus Christ. I thought of the miracles of God's love I had seen, not only this week, but down through the years.

I thought especially of that lonely night, a year before, when I had stood outside a hut in the bush country of northwest Zambia after praying unsuccessfully for a dead child to be raised to life. *"Because you have been faithful,"* the Lord had said to me, *"I will let you see great things."*

That child, I recalled, had been five years old when he died. Now, one year later, I had seen a six-year-old child, suffering from the same illness, raised from death in answer to my prayers. At the same moment, I had seen the life of my own baby son preserved by the incredible miracle-working love of God. I had done my best to be faithful, and God had been true to his word. He had let me see great things, beyond my wildest imaginings.

Truly, I thought, nothing the Lord did would ever surprise me now.

FIFTEEN

"Set the Nations Free"

"**P**LEASE, SIR. Please. Will you pray for my little girl?"

I had just finished a healing session in the Sachibandu province of northwest Zambia. I had been there for several days, ministering to some of the most destitute, most abandoned people I had ever seen. Many of them owned only the clothing they had on their backs. Most of them had no shoes. There were thousands of them, flocking in from all the villages round about, desperate to hear the Word of God and to be touched by his power.

God had honored their faith. I would lay hands on people and pray for them, and they would fall to the ground, overcome by the manifest presence and power of the Holy Spirit. One man, whose ankles had been grotesquely twisted and misshapen since birth, was instantly healed. There were many other miraculous healings, too many to count.

Now I turned to look at the woman who had called out to me. She said, "Sir, I have seen those people being healed. Would you pray for my little girl?"

"Of course," I said. "Where is she?"

The woman lifted up the hem of her dress. There, hidden under her mother's skirts, stood a little girl. She looked to be about three years old.

I knelt down to take her hand. As I coaxed her toward me, I could see ugly, red ulcers all over her body. She clearly had some terrible skin disease. It made me shiver just to look at her. I could only imagine the pain she must have been in.

Then I noticed the mother's back, where her shawl had slipped down from her shoulder. Her skin, too, was covered with sores. It looked like leprosy.

I prayed for both of them, placing my hands on their shoulders. The mother looked up at me with tears in her eyes and said, "Thank you, sir. We have had preachers come to us before, but you are the first one who has ever stepped down and touched us. Thank you for coming from America to pray for us poor people."

My own eyes filled with tears, too. Surely, I thought, the heart of God is for these people. Surely it is of such as these that the Lord Jesus spoke when he said, "The Spirit of the Lord is on me, because he has anointed me to preach good news to the poor. He has sent me to proclaim freedom for the prisoners and recovery of sight for the blind, to release the oppressed, to proclaim the year of the Lord's favor" (Lk 4:18-19).

As I walked away, I felt the Lord bring to mind the story of Elijah in the cave at Horeb (1 Kgs 19). He had run into opposition for obeying the Lord's command and had fled to this cave, where he was hiding from his enemies.

"What are you doing here, Elijah?" asked the Lord. Elijah poured out his tale of woe, trying to explain why he was hiding out in a cave. Again the Lord asked his question, and again Elijah gave his answer.

Then the Lord stopped asking questions and started giving orders: "Go back the way you came. . . ." He sent Elijah to pray for those who were to set the nation of Israel free.

Now I sensed the Lord speaking to me. "Do you feel compassion for these people?" he asked.

"Yes, sir," I said.

"The way you see these people is the way I see the nations. I feel compassion for them. They are hurting. They are hungry, like this woman, for anything they can receive from me. I want to send my church to them, to touch them, to pray for them, to feed them, to heal them. But my church is hiding as if in a cave, turning its face from the poor and the needy, hardening its heart against the nations. The anointing is there, but they do not see it. I want to use my church to set the nations free."

How many times since then have I seen this promise of God borne out! Time after time, as we bring the Word of God to the poor of the earth, the Holy Spirit comes in power. Truly the heart of God is for these people.

ME, A MISSIONARY TO AMERICA?

God has not only called me to bring his Word and healing to the poor in Third World countries. Just as I have seen many healed in Africa, so I have seen mighty manifestations of the Spirit in the United States. For instance, while ministering at the 1988 World Missions Conference for the Christian Broadcasting Network (CBN) University in Virginia Beach, Virginia, I was asked to appear on CBN's TV show "Straight Talk." During the broadcast, I received a word of knowledge that God was healing a "lady in red clothing" who suffered from terrible pain in her knees.

Later a woman called CBN from Colorado Springs, saying that she was wearing a red sweater and had been healed of a crippling case of arthritis. Weeping over the phone, the woman explained that she was no longer able to care for her children because of worsening arthritis. She reported that she had felt heat going through her knees and then the pain had left her. In all, there were nearly twenty responses from women in red clothing who said that they had experienced healing during that broadcast.

A man called and reported being healed of arthritis during that time. He had been confined to his couch because of intense pain in his knees. At the moment of feeling God's healing touch, he said that he had gone out and run up and down the front steps of his home.

I will never forget a 1986 rally in Richmond, Virginia, sponsored by New Generations Campus Ministries, which reaches over sixty black universities in America with the gospel. As I was laying hands on the leaders at the rally, a group of college students were on stage singing, about twenty feet away. I turned to look at them and they all fell off the stage, slain by the power of the Spirit.

At the same time, the wind of the Holy Spirit came on a paralyzed woman in a wheelchair. There was no draft in the auditorium, but the woman's hair was blowing. I told her, "The Holy Spirit is over you."

She replied, "I have never felt like this." Then she walked out of her wheelchair.

While it has been a great privilege to see God's healing hand at work in the United States, it was in a hotel room on March 7, 1986, in Washington, D.C. that I came to understand more fully the heart of my ministry to America.

I had just had the privilege of leading the national day of prayer and fasting for America in the House of Representatives, and had then returned to my hotel room. Suddenly, it was as if the scales fell from my eyes. As an adopted son of this nation, I hold a great debt of gratitude to America. So what God told me there in that hotel room surprised me.

"I have called you also to be a missionary to America," he said.

Me? I thought. But my heart has always been primarily with the poor and broken people of the Third World! What can I offer to America?

Then as God's purposes became clearer, he answered questions that had been with me through fourteen years of prayer and fasting. I had felt strange and alone as I endured my long and frequent fasts. Yet I knew God was compelling me to such periods of fasting and prayer.

In that hotel room, the Lord said, "I have made fasting prayer a living truth in your life. Now go through this nation to impart this gift and train the thousands I will show you. Satan wants to destroy America from the inside and has built many evil strongholds over it. [Yet] it is my will that from America a mighty thrust of the gospel go to all nations....

"Satan plans to weaken and destroy this nation. It will be the work of believers who are willing to pay the price of prayer and fasting that America will remain strong, for this kind [of evil spirit] goes not out but through prayer and fasting...."

I had prayed for fourteen years for a visitation of God in America. And in that hotel room, in the nation's capital, it all became clear. The key to victory over the evil strongholds of secular humanism, abortion, communism, drugs, divorce, pornography, child abuse, and atheism would come through spiritual warfare.

In its beginning, America was established as a land where people were invited to serve the Living God and enjoy all his benefits. Yet over the years, our security and blessings have seemingly given way to a self-centered striving for freedom without discipline and responsibility.

Is it any wonder that such striving has opened wide the floodgates to secular humanism, abortion, communism, divorce, pornography, child abuse, and atheism?

I now knew that the time had come to wield the spiritual weapons of intercession and fasting until the strongholds fell and revival came to America. It was also clear that God was commissioning me to recruit others for the fight.

As strongholds fall, I believe that one of the primary recipients of the outpouring of the Holy Spirit in America will be the black community. The conditions of life and history experienced by our black brothers and sisters have made them prime candidates for this outpouring—for he will fall upon those who are humble, holy, and hungry. Whether in Kinshasa, Zaire, Mombasa, Kenya, or Washington, D.C., those who sit in pride, thinking they are full will not necessarily get anything more from God. But for everyone who will respond humbly and obediently to his Word, God is full of love and mercy. And when the Holy Spirit comes, he will make those who were not a people become a people.

FULL CIRCLE

The journey that started for me when I wanted to cling to the proud heritage of my *Rajput* ancestors as a boy, instead of accepting the love and mercy of Jesus as my Lord and Savior, has become an amazing one, marked all along the way with "signs" of the Lord's great power and compassion.

At Easter, 1990, I held an evangelistic campaign in Chatsworth/Durban, South Africa. This East Indian township centers around the largest Hindu Krishna temple in the southern hemisphere. One million Indians live in this area. It was there, between that temple and the *Rajput* Center of Culture, that we set up a tent seating twelve thousand and proclaimed Jesus to Hindu and Moslem alike. Ten thousand people received Christ as Lord and Savior. Hundreds more were healed of incurable diseases and delivered from evil spirits.

I remember standing before that temple, the sunlight glinting from its golden domes, and recalling myself outside another temple as a boy of fourteen years, saying "God, I know you are out there somewhere, please show me." That's exactly what he has done.

My vision is to fulfill Jesus' command to take the gospel to all the earth with signs and wonders following. When people see the miracles of God in their midst, they know the message of the gospel is true. I want all men and women to be able to obey the words of Jesus: "Go back and report what you have seen and heard: The blind receive sight, the lame walk, those who have leprosy are cured, the deaf hear, the dead are raised, and the good news is preached to the poor" (Lk 7:22).

From that night in Mombasa when the Lord Jesus placed his hand on my shoulder and said, "My little brother," to the ambassadorship of love I received for the children at the State School, to the raising from the dead of Katshinyi Manikai and the conversion to Christ of thousands around the world, I have seen Jesus perform signs and wonders of every kind. In the same way that I have experienced him as ultimate truth, I have experienced Jesus as ultimate love. I have come to know that only love can make a miracle.

COME VISIT US!

**Chavda Ministries International
All Nations Church
Watch of the Lord™ World Headquarters:
360 Hammond Rd., Fort Mill, South Carolina**

SUNDAY MORNING SERVICE: 10:00 AM (EST)
**Spirit-filled worship plus anointed teaching by Mahesh and
Bonnie Chavda. Healing and prophetic ministry every service.**

FRIDAY NIGHT WATCH: 7:30 PM (EST)
**Lively and anointed extended worship and prayer. Ministry
of the Word, healing, and prophetic ministry every service.**

**For updates, resources, testimonies, articles, information on our
conferences and events, or to join us live, visit us online at:
www.chavdaministries.org**

**Chavda Ministries International
PO Box 411008
Charlotte, NC 28241
Phone: (704) 543-7272 or (800) 730-6264
Fax: (704) 541-5300
Email: info@chavdaministries.org
www.chavdaministries.org**